GREEN

Also available from Souvenir Press

Health and Nutrition
THE FOOD MEDICINE BIBLE by Earl Mindell
THE ANTI-AGEING BIBLE by Earl Mindell
WHEAT-FREE COOKING by Rita Greer
ANTIOXIDANT NUTRITION by Rita Greer and Dr Robert Woodward
THE BOOK OF VITAMINS AND HEALTHFOOD SUPPLEMENTS by Rita Greer and Dr Robert Woodward
RITA GREER'S VEGETARIAN COOKBOOK by Rita Greer
THE HAY DIET MADE EASY by Jackie Habgood
THE OSTEOPOROSIS PREVENTION GUIDE by Dr Sarah Brewer
SOFT OPTIONS by Rita Greer
GET WELL WITH THE HAY DIET by Jackie Habgood
PREGNANCY THE NATURAL WAY by Dr Sarah Brewer

Nature's Remedies
GINGER by Dr Stephen Fulder
OLIVE OIL by Rita Greer and Cyril Blau
ALOE VERA by Alasdair Barcroft
LAVENDER by Philippa Waring
GINKGO AND GARLIC by Nicola Peterson
SAW PALMETTO by Dr Ray Sahelian
ECHINACEA by Douglas Schar
HYPERICUM by Andrew Chevallier
SAGE by Penelope Ody

NATURE'S REMEDIES

GREEN TEA

Good Health in Your Cup

Diana Rosen

SOUVENIR PRESS

Copyright © 1998 by Diana Rosen

The right of Diana Rosen to be identified as author of this work has been asserted by her in accordance with the Copyright, Designs and Patents Act 1988.

The diagram on p.89 is by Carol Jessop.
Aubrey's Green Tea Moisturiser recipe is reprinted with permission from *The Take Charge Beauty Book* by Aubrey Hampton and Susan Hussey, Kensington Publishing, New York, 1999.

First published in the USA by
Storey Books, Inc., Pownal, Vermont
under the title *The Book of Green Tea*

First British edition published 2000 by
Souvenir Press Ltd.,
43 Great Russell Street, London WC1B 3PA

All Rights Reserved. No part of this publication may be reproduced, stored in a retrieval system or transmitted, in any form or by any means, electronic, mechanical, photocopying, recording or otherwise, without the prior permission of the Copyright owner.

ISBN 0 285 63556 5

Typeset by Rowland Phototypesetting Ltd.,
Bury St Edmunds, Suffolk

Printed in Great Britain by The Guernsey Press Co. Ltd.,
Guernsey, Channel Islands

To all the men and women
who plant, harvest and process
the teas of the world.
All the pleasure of *Camellia sinensis* begins with you.

Acknowledgements

For their particular expertise in tea growing, processing, and the cultures of China, India, Sri Lanka, Taiwan and Vietnam, I would like to thank:
Swaraj Kumar 'Rajah' Banerjee, Makaibari Tea Estates, Darjeeling, India
Stephen Chao and staff, Eastrise Tea Corporation, Alhambra, California
Roy Fong, Imperial Tea Court, San Francisco, California
Manik Jayakumar, Q-Trade International, Rancho Santa Margarita, California
Gabriella Karsch, The Indochina Tea Co., Studio City, California
Anupa Mueller, Eco-Prima, Ossining, New York
Lalith Paranavitana, Empire Tea Services, Columbus, Indiana
Dan Robertson, The Teahouse, Naperville, Illinois
Devan Shah, India Tea Importers, Montebello, California

For research, advice, tea, critiques, referrals, translations, and so much more, I thank the following incredibly generous and gracious people: James Burnett, Ecology Works, Forest Knolls, California; Kit Chow, author of *All the Tea in China*; Paul Hilderbrandt, Tokyo, Japan, for Japanese translations; Bob Jones, for Chinese translations; Hasan Mukhtar, Ph.D., Professor and Director of Research, Department of Dermatology, Case Western Reserve University, Cleveland, Ohio, and author of nearly 40 professional papers on green tea and health, for input into the health benefits of green tea; Bill Todd, Todd & Holland Tea Merchants, River Forest, Illinois; Chef Robert Wemischner, Los Angeles, California, for creative and fabulously delicious recipes made with green tea.

I also thank dear friends and cheerleaders Karen Benke, Suzanne J. Brown, William E. Johnston Jr., Dona Schweiger, and Karen

Strange and the staff of The Writers' Mill Valley Store, California, for always soothing me while solving a computer crisis; and my agent, Mr William J. Birnes.

Note to Readers

The aim of this book is to provide information on green tea—as a refreshing drink, as a preventative and in the treatment of relevant diseases. Although every care has been taken to ensure that the advice is accurate and practical, it is not intended to be a guide to self-diagnosis and self-treatment. Where health is concerned—and in particular a serious problem of any kind—it must be stressed that there is no substitute for seeking advice from a qualified medical or herbal practitioner. All persistent symptoms, of whatever nature, may have underlying causes that need, and should not be treated without, professional elucidation and evaluation.

It is therefore very important, if you are considering trying green tea for medicinal purposes, to consult your practitioner first, and if you are already taking any prescribed medication, do not stop it.

The Publisher makes no representation, express or implied, with regard to the accuracy of the information contained in this book, and legal responsibility or liability cannot be accepted by the Author or the Publisher for any errors or omissions that may be made or for any loss, damage, injury or problems suffered or in any way arising from following the advice offered in these pages.

Contents

	Acknowledgements	7
	Note to Readers	9
1	The Poetry of Green Tea	13
2	History and Lore	17
3	Processing Tea	28
4	China Teas (Cha)	32
5	Indian Teas (Chai)	45
6	Japanese Teas (O-cha)	52
7	Other Sources of Green Tea	58
8	Buying, Storing and Brewing	66
9	Serving	72
10	Wellness	82
11	Beauty and Health	91
12	Green Tea in Cooking	100
	Glossary	112
	Resources	117
	Recommended Reading	123

CHAPTER 1

The Poetry of Green Tea

Tea is drunk to forget the din of the world.
T'ien Yiheng

Green tea, my friends, is poetry.

True, oolong tea can be more fragrant than the finest French perfume. And black teas are legendary, as comforting by the hearth on a cold winter's day as they are charming subjects in hundreds, nay, thousands of pages of great literature.

The intentionally aged, digestive pu-erh is soothing and more healthful than a midnight glass of warmed milk. The yellows, while still rather rare, are divine, each one tasted immediately placed in our life memory box. And the whites are exquisite examples of how even the little unopened bud leaf can deliver brews to dream about.

This book, however, is all about the tea of the ancients that is as modern as today, that delicate, ephemeral, almost-there quality of the finest green tea.

'Real' tea

I began my life in tea like most Americans do, thinking of 'real' tea as that golden-red liquid into which one pours a dollop of milk and a spoonful or more of sugar. As my circle of tea acquaintances grew, I was introduced to tea 'plain', quickly embracing the briskness of a Ceylon, the dark sweetness of a Yunnan black, the complexity of a genuine single-estate Darjeeling.

By great fortune, my first experiences with green tea were absolutely ideal: introduced by an avid and experienced Chinese teaman who served me in his own authentic Chinese teahouse. Tea was offered in a covered cup, curved inwards slightly to fit even the smallest hands, and placed atop a matching saucer that kept the hot cup from harming the hands. A domed lid was used as a paddle to push the fresh green leaves back and forth until they gave up their sweetness and provided me with their ambrosial nectar.

I was in love. I quickly and enthusiastically embraced the Chinese styles of preparation, acquiring the accoutrements one by one until my tea cabinet was full of their beauty.

The more I drank green tea, the more appreciative I was. The more varieties I experienced, the more astonished I became that this innocent leaf could be dried, steamed or lightly pan-fired, and shaped in countless ways, always with the same result—pure pleasure. It was easy to understand the teaman's demands for beauty in the dried state and in the infused leaf.

The everyday pleasure of tea

Of the Chinese, you might ask, 'Have you leisure time to have tea with me?' The result will be relaxed, happy hours drinking your favourite teas while talking, perhaps engaging in a clattering mah-jongg game or listening to finches chirping sweetly as they swing in bamboo cages hanging from the ceiling of the teahouse. If you are really fortunate, you may stumble into a teahouse where traditional storytellers spin their centuries-old tales, which are sometimes more intoxicating than wine!

For the Japanese, green tea is an everyday pleasure drunk with morning rice (or even poured over it), served with other meals and to visitors, and on important occasions, served much more elegantly at the formal tea ceremony called *chanoyu*. This way of tea never ceases to transport me, to offer a long-lasting spiritual vacation, to bring me to a place of calm and serene attitude that derives solely from watching the ballet of *chanoyu*, in which the simplicity of water and leaf is elevated to pure art.

For the Vietnamese, Nepalese, Indonesians, and those in other tea-growing countries in the Pacific Rim, green tea is the everyday tea, ranging from the straightforward, even blunt taste of a roughly processed green to that world of savouring just beyond exquisite that comes from drinking the most cherished, most tenderly handled teas in the world.

To the Indians and Sri Lankans, especially those dedicated to organic tea farming, their green teas bring many health-giving properties and nearly infinite tasting pleasures, without sacrificing the indescribable qualities that makes the Indian and Ceylon teas endlessly satisfying to the palate.

What is tea?

What is tea to me? Tea is an olfactory experience; its aroma can be clean and pungent, sweet and soft. All the wonderful aromas can carry you to a place of greater calm and peace.

Tea is a retreat in a cup. Tea is quite literally 'therapy in a cup', a way to sort out, think through, resolve to do. Tea gives you permission to relax, to be in the moment, and to be truly who you are.

Tea is the most intimate of beverages. To truly appreciate tea, you need to sit down and be introspective. Within moments, you will have greater clarity of thought and a clearer sense of purpose. It is just you, your thoughts, and the magic of a bowl of tea.

Tea requires time. If you give enough quality time to tea, it will reward you with more than you ever imagined. You can get lost in tea. You can find yourself in tea. In fact, I had better warn you now: tea can change your life.

The health benefits of green tea

But is tea only for pleasure? Happily, I can say tea is not only enjoyable, it's good for you. For centuries, China has praised the health benefits of its native plant. Scientists around the world have researched and examined the leaf exhaustively, and feel they now know some of the 'why' that makes this simple beverage do so much. Tea provides benefits for bones and teeth. Its vital chemical compounds have been found to fight cancer, help stabilise diabetes and do much to prevent cardiovascular disease. It even makes your skin healthier and prettier.

You can drink it, use it for medication, cook with it; you can even water your plants and keep your cat's litter tray fresh and pleasant-smelling with it.

And the most beneficial, most healthful tea is the barely processed leaf from the *Camellia sinensis* bush—green tea. How does a brew from one plant do so much?

That is our story. May this book bring you information pure and simple, pleasures small and great.

CHAPTER 2

History and Lore

Better to be deprived of food for three days than tea for one.
Ancient Chinese saying

While 'modern' history certainly includes the growth of the tea industry in India, and although wild tea plants have been discovered in the contiguous areas of south-west China, Burma and India, most historians and botanists now believe the tea plant first began in China. It was most likely brought to India, Korea, Sri Lanka and Japan by monks, who enthusiastically embraced it as a way to stay alert during their hours-long meditations. Still, the legends—and some noteworthy recorded accounts—prevail to tickle our imagination and tweak our curiosity.

The story of Sh'eng Nung

Ever since the Emperor Sh'eng Nung allegedly took the first sip of tea in about 2737 BC, man has made tea the second most popular beverage after water (one-fifth of all tea drunk in the world is green tea). What the emperor first tasted was unwithered and unadulterated—pure tea in every sense of the word.

The legend goes that the emperor was relaxing outdoors under a tree, royally napping as it were, listening to the perky bubbling of the small cauldron of water over a nearby fire. (The ancient Chinese fully understood the value and health-giving properties of freshly boiled water.) A gentle breeze wafted through the nearby trees, carrying with it a few leaves, which casually dropped into the boiling water.

A less curious person would simply have thrown out the leaves or considered them a nuisance, but the emperor was intrigued by the aroma that resulted from this unexpected marriage of leaf and water. Ever game, he scooped a little of the leaf-spotted water into a small cup, and dared a sip. Then another, and another. Soon he sent his servant to fetch more leaves, and a new beverage was born from this tree we now know as *Camellia sinensis*, an evergreen bush related to the flowering camellia that can grow to great heights.

The emperor's story is thought to be purely legend because the tea plants of Sh'eng Nung's era were largely unknown before the Han era (202 BC—AD 220) and only first noted in the *Pen T'sao* (third century AD). It mentions the 'bitter tasting tu from the hills of Ichow', which was good for abscesses in the head and 'which diminishes the desire for sleep'. The Chinese ideogram for *tu* is also now known to be incorrect, although for centuries it was attributed to no less a scholar than Confucius. It is now believed that tu was an herbaceous plant.

There is, however, some evidence that the emperor was actually quite educated in the plants of his country. Instead of the casual curiosity always attributed to him in stories, it was more likely keen scholarly interest that led him to experiment with tea leaves and water. So ardent a plant enthusiast was he that he is said to have introduced herbal medicine and agriculture to Chinese society.

Boiling water as art

In the Shang period (1760–1122 BC) tea was definitely used as a medicine, but it was not until the Han era that it was used as a beverage. As a popular drink, it gained its first really enthusiastic reaction during the Sung dynasty (AD 960–1279), when even boiling water was elevated to an art, and competitions were occasionally held by friends of the court to display their skill at tea-making and boiling water exactly to suit the teas.

During that era, tea was not brewed as loose leaves but rolled into balls. For competitions, contestants would scratch residue from these balls, then the cleaned balls were ground into a powder and placed into striking black glazed bowls from the famous Jian kilns in the province of Fujian. Hot water was poured on the tea, which was then stirred into a white frothy foam—hence a sharp contrast to the dramatic black bowls.

The contestant whose foam lasted the longest won, with much credit given to those who had bigger and higher foam. The tea water had to be clear, though. If it was green, the steaming and cooking process had begun. It couldn't be grey—an indication of overstirring and overcooking. It couldn't be yellow, either, for that indicated the leaves had not been fresh enough.

Tea the beverage

The competition for creative frothing with boiling water soon gave way to a deeper appreciation of tea as a beverage. Green tea was and is today the most popular type of tea drunk in China. For centuries, until the Ming dynasty (AD 1368–1644), it was actually the only type of tea produced in its homeland.

Today, there is not just one green tea but hundreds, and many varieties have several grades of quality. This intoxicating group of choices is further enhanced by the changes, from season to season, of the quality of teas. That can make savouring green tea similar to wine connoisseurship—a particular harvest may produce spectacular grapes one year and mediocre ones the next. But, unlike wine, green tea has a very short life span and must be consumed quickly or it will lose colour, aroma and, more importantly, flavour.

The T'ang dynasty (AD 618–907) was the time in which tea was first recognised and accepted as a beverage rather than a medicine. In a lovely marriage of art and function, the T'ang era also brought the development and perfection of porcelain-making. The delicacy of celadon and white porcelain for tea bowls gained so much popularity that many innovations were designed to satisfy the growing number of tea drinkers eager to show off their tea-making expertise. One new design was the saucer, a convenient and clever way to protect hands from a hot cup. The T'ang era produced many of the great poets of tea and, alas, the initial taxation on tea—but that, as the saying goes, is another story.

First record of tea

In addition to our gratitude to the Chinese for experimenting with this combination of leaf and water and for the art of porcelain-making, we must also be thankful to them for the invention of the tools and techniques for writing things down in such a way that scholarly texts exist today, tracing the earliest records of tea.

A contract for slaves written by Wang Pao, poet laureate to Emperor Husan, includes a written notation of the exact date of the first mention of tea in China: 18 February, 59 BC. The contract, known as 'Tan Yuch', is also one of the earliest recorded mentions of tea in any form.

In another famous early tract, *The History of the Three Kingdoms* by Chang Hua (AD 232–300), the tale of Wei Chao is described. A particular favourite at court but a man indisposed to drinking, Chao never could manage to consume the required seven *sheng* (vessels) of wine, despite strong orders from the emperor that he do so.

Thinking himself very clever, Chao finally discovered a solution to his social faux pas, and substituted tea for the wine. Despite his valiant efforts to save himself from debauchery, his subterfuge was uncovered, and he was executed in AD 273 for this infraction against the royal house.

In the writings of Chinese scholar Kuo P'o in the ancient dictionary known as *Erh Ya* (AD 359), there are several references to a medicinal beverage made by boiling raw green leaves. This beverage, called k'utu, must have tasted quite bitter, as the leaves were completely unprocessed—neither steamed, dried nor roasted in any way. (It may also have been not tea at all but tu, the medicinal herbaceous plant.)

Some herbalists who championed the use of tea leaves as medicine created many innovative ways to use it in their treatments. One popular recipe for soothing stomach disorders of patients was to press the tea leaves into cakes and roast them, then boil the cakes with health-giving ginger and onion.

When tea's various pleasures as a beverage were finally discovered and appreciated, it quickly became something only royalty could have; it was much later on that tea trickled down, so to speak, to the masses.

The origins of tea India style

To be sure, we have only legends to guide us to the 'truth about tea'. One Buddhist legend tells of the journey between India and China in reverse order. A Chinese scholar named Gan Lu visited India, where he came to embrace Buddhism. Upon his return to China, he brought back not only this new religion, but also the beginning of a new crop: tea seeds, which he allegedly brought from the Assam area. There's just one snag to this story—Gan Lu was born *after* tea became a popular beverage in China.

India attributes the discovery of tea to the Buddhist monk Siddhartha, or Bodhidharma, in the sixth century AD. The story of this prince-turned-monk tells how he left India on his way north to preach Buddhism, vowing never to sleep during his self-imposed nine-year meditation. He reached Canton, China, in AD 519, where this 'White Buddha' remained before a wall of meditation for years.

Stalwart in his duties, he nonetheless was overwhelmed with lassitude and drowsiness at the end of only five years. By pure divine intervention, he picked and chewed leaves from an unidentified tree, and found to his delight that he had a great sense of alertness and well-being. The tree, of course, was the tea bush, and its health-giving properties allowed him to keep his vow.

Another story also attributes the discovery of tea to the prince, but this is a harsher version of the legend. At the end of only three years of meditation, the prince fell asleep, 'dreaming of all the women he had ever loved'. Despite the pleasure of the dream, he awakened furious with himself for having slept. Thinking this an unforgivable weakness, he tore off his eyelids and buried them in the ground beside the tree where he had rested, and set off to preach his religion to anyone he could influence.

Returning to the same spot months later, he discovered his eyelids had taken root and grown into a verdant bush, the like of which he had never seen before. Curious, he chewed some of the leaves and found that they helped to keep him alert. Enthusiastic about this discovery, he told his followers about this 'wonder tree' and they proceeded to gather seeds from the new bush. They cultivated tea in the nearby regions and tea became an enormously popular beverage everywhere his followers went.

The prince himself continued his journey and brought tea to Japan, where this health-giving beverage was also quickly embraced by monks, who used the tea to keep alert during their own meditations.

The British grow tea in India

From the mid-seventeenth century until the nineteenth, Britain imported all her tea from China, but two Scotsmen were to change all that. The man usually credited with 'discovering' wild tea plants growing in the Indian province of Assam is Major Robert Bruce, who in 1823 found Indian tea bushes growing on both sides of the Brahmaputra River. The area had the right combination of climate, alluvial soil along the river banks, and other factors of topography that have since contributed to the strong production Assam has enjoyed. Lovers of Assam tea say it has 'the strength to cure your weakness'.

Bruce also found that these tea bushes had a completely different appearance from the Chinese tea plants, although they were and are definitely part of the same species, *Camellia sinensis assamica*. Chinese plants have thin, small leaves and Assam plants have large, broad leaves; compared to Chinese bushes, it takes about half as many pluckings to make a pound of dried tea.

At first under government initiative, an area of forest was cleared and the huge plantations begun which today produce about 250 million kilograms of tea in Assam—about one-third of India's entire crop. The first tea from these early plantations was auctioned in London in January 1839, and in the same year the privately funded Assam Company took over their running and development.

The tea plants in the rest of India, which appear to be descendants of Chinese bushes, were those stealthily acquired by Scottish botanist Robert Fortune, sent as a 'spy' by the venerable East India

HISTORY AND LORE

Company in 1848. Having previously spent nearly three years in China on a plant-hunting expedition for the Horticultural Society in London, he had become so familiar with the area that he was able to dress and style himself to look Chinese and so infiltrate the finest tea-growing areas.

His professional education enabled him to take just the right cuttings. We're not talking about a few sprigs, either; he somehow managed to acquire more than 23,000 young plants and 17,000 seedlings, a 'quantity of manufacturing implements' and 'eight experienced Chinese teamen' whose transfer he supervised to the tea plantations forming in India. Legend has it that Fortune, with his entourage, walked—literally—the treacherous, hazardous journey from China to India with the precious cargo that helped India become the largest grower of tea in the world.

Over many years in the early 1800s, more than a million plants had been transported to India by other agents for the East India Company, but many thousands of these plants died en route. Fortune was just one among many, yet certainly one of the more successful ones.

His achievements are remembered primarily because he set his recollections down in an engaging style in several books which became best-sellers of the time. These books read like fictional travelogues, tales of 'Indiana Jones' adventuring, plus some genuinely important (and importantly genuine) personal accounts of what tea cultivation was really like in China in the nineteenth century.

Among his most popular books are *Three Years' Wanderings in the Northern Provinces of China including a Visit to the Tea, Silk and Cotton Countries* (1847); *A Journey to the Tea Countries of China Including Sung-Lo and the Bohea Hills* (1852), and *Two Visits to the Tea Countries of China and the British Tea Plantations of the Himalayas* (1853). They were published by John Murray of London, and some remaining copies are still available in libraries devoted to botany and Chinese agriculture.

The British government was delighted to see a popular and profitable crop of tea growing in India, where many of the 'British' customs of tea service were quickly adopted. Independent of mother England for more than fifty years, India nonetheless still brews and serves tea 'English' style, except for the uniquely Indian drink called *masala chai* —a hearty mixture of milk, tea and spices such as cardamom, cinnamon and pepper.

The Japanese tradition

Tea in Japan, as in China, was first used as a medicine more than as a beverage of refreshment. Historical records cite the existence of powdered tea called *hiki-cha* (a very rough powdered tea, similar to matcha—see p. 27), which was bestowed upon priests summoned to the court of the Japanese Emperor Shomu in about AD 729. The teas, rare and costly even then, were well received by the 100 priests reading scriptures at the imperial palace, and when they returned to their own monasteries they began to grow tea for themselves in temple gardens.

One of the most famous stories about the introduction of tea to Japan is that of the Buddhist monk Dengyo Daishi (Saicho) who had spent time in China from AD 803–805. He noticed the way the Chinese monks stayed alert during their meditations as a result of drinking tea. Realising the benefits of this beverage, Daishi enthusiastically brought back tea plantings to his emperor, Saga, who encouraged the cultivation of this new plant, thus bringing tea to millions of Japanese.

What transpired during the three centuries after Daishi's time is a little vague. We do know that by the twelfth century tea was cultivated in the Uji district not far from Kyoto (the ancient capital of Japan), and Uji remains a premier tea-growing area.

How that cultivation was made possible is a continuing story. Although it could have been from Daishi's original efforts, another story contends that tea was cultivated from seeds brought to Japan by another renowned Zen Buddhist priest and teacher, Eisai (Yei-sai), who lived from 1141–1215.

When Eisai went to China in 1187, he returned with Buddhist inspiration and more tea seeds, which were first planted in Uji. Fortunately for future generations, he wrote about these efforts to plant, harvest and use tea in a book, *Kitcha Yojoki*, or 'Maintaining

Health by Drinking Tea', also known as *The Book of Tea Sanitation*. Published in 1211, it was the first work on tea written in Japan, and did much to foster Eisai's own personal beliefs that tea had medicinal qualities and could be used to treat a number of diseases.

Tea drinking was thoroughly and consistently embraced by Buddhist monks, who developed a simple drinking ceremony in which tea played a critical role in making this a spiritual experience. Zen priests travelled throughout Asia bringing their messages of peace and, naturally, were instrumental in bringing both their religion and tea to Japan.

Many important Zen Buddhist teachers contributed to the evolution of the tea ceremony over several generations, but it is largely the contributions of three particular teachers which are cited as most outstanding to the refinement of chanoyu as we know it today—and to the slow but eventual introduction of this ceremony to all strata of Japanese life.

The first was Ikkyu (1394–1481), a former prince, who was able to influence others in the royal court to participate in this levelling experience called the tea ceremony. He turned over his leadership to one of his prized students, Murata Shuko (1422–1502), who did much during his lifetime to foster and sustain interest in the Japanese tea ceremony.

It was largely Sen-no Rikyu (1521–1591), however, who set the standards of what we now know as chanoyu. The son of a wealthy merchant in the city of Sakai, he became a friend and confidant of several shoguns, most notably Toyotomi Hideyoshi.

Their relationship enabled Rikyu to encourage other military leaders to embrace the emerging tea culture. Shogun Hideyoshi became an ardent patron of the art of tea, and it was his approval that did so much to catapult the tea ceremony into general acceptance—and importance—among warlords.

Before long, it was customary for warlords to pause for tea before each important battle, and to incorporate much of its philosophy into their lives. Alas, Shogun Hideyoshi eventually revealed his deepest despotic feelings and ordered Rikyu to commit suicide.

Who knows what greater heights chanoyu would have achieved had Rikyu lived longer than his fruitful seventy years?

Chanoyu
Tea master Sen-no Rikyu brought an unusual combination of poetry and philosophy to the art of tea. As a result, he is credited with doing the most to formalise and ritualise chanoyu into the serene combination of art, poetry and aesthetics that it is today. Rikyu established at least three schools of chanoyu, and over the centuries the most formal of these has been honed by subsequent tea masters into one of the most elegant and serene ways of serving tea.

For both the host and the guests, the many restrictions on etiquette and performance keep the focus of everyone on the central element of the experience: the tea. This concentration also gives participants the ability to genuinely relax, to experience freedom from worldly cares, to embrace the sense of peace that can be enjoyed over a bowl of tea.

From its inception, chanoyu promoted composure with the performance of each function conducted with absolute care, so that each act would teach precision, poise, tranquillity, courtesy, sincerity, unselfishness and daintiness. The result would be harmony in one's life, in every sense, for both the host and the guests.

Most rooms for chanoyu are about three metres (nine feet) square, and covered with tatami mats, each 1×2 metres (3×6 feet) in size, a concept developed by Ashikaga Yoshimasa in the fifteenth century. Although the sizes and shapes of tea rooms have evolved over the years, the basic principal elements remain: a low door for all to enter at the same level (head bowed down) so no one is considered more important than another; an alcove for a singular piece of art—a scroll with beautiful calligraphy, an arrangement of exquisite flowers (or more often, a single flower), or a piece of art—a painting, ceramic, or small hand-painted screen.

Other objects in the room are for the preparation of the tea itself: a brazier for heating the water and a simple shelf for the main accessories such as the ladle, bowls, and caddy filled with tea. Sometimes, either inside the room or just outside it, another shelf discreetly holds accessories or the foods served during the ceremony.

The tea for chanoyu is matcha, made from Japan's finest tea leaves—gyokuro, or 'precious dew'—which are dried and ground into a brilliant, silky, chartreuse powder. Stirred with hot water into the consistency of thick pea soup, a bowl of this tea is set gracefully in front of each guest, who then drinks from it while holding the bowl with both hands. Sometimes sweets, made of red bean paste or other delicately flavoured ingredients, are served on small plates and eaten with the fingers. The sweetness counteracts any bitterness of the matcha; however, the finest matcha is itself rather sweet in its frothiness and is very pleasant tasting.

In other Japanese tea ceremonies, usually less complex and less structured, the hosts use a green tea from the Uji district near Kyoto, which is prepared especially for each guest. Although service is always elegant and restrained, it does not include all the elaborate steps of a traditional chanoyu.

Some twenty-four schools of tea grew out of this enthusiasm for tea drinking in Japan, and today the Urasenke school is undoubtedly the most popular. Urasenke schools are located in Britain and Canada, and in the United States locations are open in Washington, DC, Seattle, Honolulu, San Francisco and New York. The headquarters for Urasenke Konnichian, named for one of the founding teachers, are in Kyoto, Japan. The foundation was established by Tea Master Konnichian in 1964 to encourage good will via the cultural exchange 'over a bowl of tea'. The public can attend seasonal tea gatherings or begin the lifelong study of this beautifully wrought tradition from the seventeenth century.

CHAPTER 3

Processing Tea

Come oh come ye tea-thirsty restless ones—the kettle boils, bubbles, and sings musically.
Rabindranath Tagore (1861–1941)

There are many variations in processing depending upon the country—China, Japan, India, Taiwan, Sri Lanka and others—but the principles of the process remain the same: precisely engineered machinery operated under careful management, or, for the finest teas, hand-drying, firing and rolling.

Harvesting tea

Harvesting tea is the beginning of the journey of leaf to cup. Only the top two leaves and the leaf bud are plucked for their tenderness, their fullness of flavour, and their ability to be twisted or rolled into a variety of shapes. This precision hand-plucking requires dexterity and concentration, and must be done while enduring heat, altitude and long hours. Tea-plucking is, for the most part, women's work—and hard work at that.

Each plucker must carry a large basket on her back, protect her head from the increasingly warm sun, and employ both stamina and agility to pluck only certain leaves of each bush, working at good speed for hours on end. In India, Sri Lanka and China, most tea pluckers live right where they farm. One exception is Kenya, where the tea farms are often miles away from the villages. So it is men who do the plucking in Kenya, for they must stay on the farms for days or weeks until the job is done—an acceptable arrangement for men to undertake but not, in their culture, considered appropriate for women.

PROCESSING TEA

Plucking is done up to four times a year depending on the geographical location, and, like all things that grow, tea is dependent upon the care and attention of the farmer and the whim of the weather. Recognising the tremendous effort of such workers can only make one more appreciative of the final cup, full of its inviting fragrance, beautiful colour and delicate taste.

Withering, pan-firing and steaming

After the tea leaves are plucked, they must be dried. The heat destroys the natural enzyme in all tea leaves. These complex proteins are present in plant cells and serve as a catalyst for chemical reactions from heat or cold. Heat prevents oxidation of polyphenols, the antioxidants that help protect against disease, yet preserves the flavonols that give tea its unique crisp taste.

Withering is a process in which the tea leaves are usually spread out on racks of bamboo or woven straw and exposed to sunlight or warm air while constantly being moved about to ensure even drying.

Pan-firing stabilises the fragrance and flavour, and, at this point, the leaves can change colour slightly. Chinese greens are softer in colour than Japanese and can be grey-green, soft yellow and green, white and green, pale green or dark green.

In China, green teas are frequently pan-fired in very large woks, many of them placed on a simple flame as they have been used for centuries. Some pan-firing is done in electric woks, which provide a stabilised temperature. With incredible deftness, the teamen push the leaves from side to side in the wok, tossing, scooping and turning them over—with a grace and skill that only experienced human hands can offer—until the leaves are evenly and completely dried.

One Chinese Long Jing (Dragonwell) processor, for example, will do eight exact movements over and over until the results he or she wants are achieved. Another processor will do ten exact movements. For Chinese green tea processors in other regions, the steps are fewer or greater, more elaborate or more simple, and largely proprietary to that region, that farmer, that processor. That's still another factor that makes Chinese luxury green teas so special. When processing is done by hands that wither, dry and shape leaves, an extra added element, the spirit and knowledge of generations, blesses every leaf.

Steaming is used to prevent oxidation and make green tea leaves more pliable for shaping. It is the typical method in Japan, where it is often done in a bamboo tray over water. Sometimes a revolving steaming machine or belt-conveyer steaming machine is used, which completes the entire process in only one or two minutes.

The craft of shaping tea leaves
In most countries, rolling or shaping green tea leaves into different shapes is done by machinery. Most top-quality green tea leaves in China, however, are hand-rolled into various shapes: curly, twisted, pointed, round, and hundreds more shapes. Rolling the tea leaves is done not just to create a decorative look but to regulate the release of natural substances and flavour when they are steeped in the cup.

With pure artistry and nimble fingers, the teamen take thousands of leaves and shape them with consummate skill and great speed. After shaping, the teas are then sorted according to size and set aside for weighing and packaging. Throughout every step of each process, particularly in China, it is the human touch that makes for the beautiful shapes of top-quality green teas. This can only come when the leaves are processed by people using an innate sense of art that goes beyond craft.

In Japan, the tea leaves are hand- or machine-rolled, and dried to the point where they can accommodate pressure for the mechanical rolling process. Using weights, the machines roll the leaves until they are various shapes and completely dried. Further refining is done to remove debris, stems and broken leaves, and then they are usually refined by human hands that sort the leaves again by size and shape.

Most Japanese tea masters agree that body temperature is the optimum temperature for rolling tea leaves, but this may vary slightly—only one or two degrees—depending on the type of tea, the location of the tea farm, or the time of day the rolling occurs.

PROCESSING TEA

Adding the scent of flowers
During the drying process, flowers are sometimes added to infuse the tea with a scent. One of the most popular flowers used in China is the night-blooming jasmine. Every evening, up to eleven nights for high-grade teas, the flowers are laid upon the green tea, left overnight and removed in the morning. The process is repeated until the natural scent of jasmine permeates the leaves, creating a green tea with an exquisite perfume and a clear, pale, delicate flavour.

In China, other flowers have been used for centuries to scent black teas or *pu-erhs*. They include the chrysanthemum, the *gui hua* or osmanthus (the delicately scented Chinese orange blossom), or rose. Sometimes fragrant lychee fruit is added.

In Japan, adding the scent of flowers to green tea is not as common as it is in China, but the results can be equally exotic. The most frequently used flowers are the cherry blossoms or delicate roses, and the most commonly used tea is sencha, after it has been steamed, dried, and shaped into its long elegant leaves.

CHAPTER 4

China Teas (Cha)

Even though one studies the tea industry until old age, one can never learn all the names of types of teas.

Fujian saying

Although cuttings from Chinese tea bushes have made their way all around the world, the peculiarities of soil, weather and attentive farming make many differences, as does altitude, which remains a dramatic and crucial factor in the cultivation of most fine teas.

Distinct aroma and appearance

Mainland China's green tea is the most delicate of all, offering a sweetness and a mild grassy taste that is satisfying, refreshing, and endlessly complex. Some Chinese green tea is astringent, like all tea can be, but generally it is very palatable, cleansing and tasty. I suspect that overastringent tea is more often the result of oversteeping than the tea leaves themselves.

The aroma of Chinese green tea can be quite intense, with fresh, sweet undertones that extend the drinking experience. Of course, the better the quality of the tea, the more infusions one can derive from any one serving of tea leaves. It is not unusual, for example, for one serving of fine Dragonwell to result in four, five, or more infusions.

Although the better quality green teas will allow more infusions, even some of the most exceptional high-quality teas do not last very long. Second and third infusions will not taste like the first, yet they can be pure elixir.

CHINA TEAS (CHA)

Processing makes the difference
Perhaps the most marked difference between Chinese greens and those grown in any other country is how the green leaves are processed. Much of the processing in mainland China is still done with painstaking handwork, from the firing in the wok or drying in the sun to the hand-twisting or rolling and the hand-sorting of the dried leaves for size and uniformity. Most of the smaller farms in China still do all processing by hand, but more and more are turning to machinery to assist them in the huge task of processing millions of kilos of teas.

As with any product, those made by hand are infused with the genuineness and that extra something that only a human being can bring to his or her work. The subtle nuances developed by master teamen and teawomen are so valuable that many people feel these tea artists should be named among China's national treasures.

One of the pleasures, and the ironies, of hand-processed teas is that no two pluckings ever generate exactly the same cup. No matter how dedicated the tea farmer, the processing of his teas today will never be exactly like it was yesterday, or exactly how it will be tomorrow. This is particularly true in the legions of tiny plots of Chinese tea farms that yield remarkable teas, many of them processed as greens.

A farmer can pluck ten kilos of leaves during the warm morning mist and process them that afternoon using centuries-old techniques of air-drying, pan-firing, or steam-drying. He will then hand-roll the leaves into signature shapes and sort them by size. The next day he may pluck another ten kilos and do the same work in the very same way, but the teas will taste slightly different. Is one cup better? Just different? Will we ever have quite that taste again? That, dear readers, is just part of the lure of tea.

The selling of Chinese green teas

As with every product today, marketing plays a great part in both the romance and the direct selling of products. Teas are no exception. Every effort has been made in this book to differentiate between names that are created solely for drama or marketing, and true names of teas, many of which have become classics over the years. Wherever possible, contemporary pinyin spellings of Chinese names have been used. Some anglicised Wade-Giles spellings—which were introduced by two British scholars in the nineteenth century—are included because they have become generic spellings in catalogues of teas, despite the trend towards pinyin and towards English names that are often romantic translations of the original Chinese names.

While it is true that some merchants have exclusives, often buying an entire year's crop (which can be as small as one kilo), most Chinese teas sold in the West are from well-established sources and fall into specific identifiable categories. Even though grades vary enormously, the leaves from the same region will definitely have that region's 'taste' in the cup. These teas may also vary in taste from year to year, but that is always considered by tea lovers one of the fascinations that keep them seeking the next cup.

Some teas are intentionally processed to be 'look-alikes' and may indeed taste wonderful, but they are not the real thing; you should not be charged the same prices as for superior grades. Always ask your tea merchant to identify the tea's origin, how it was processed and if it goes by any other name. If he or she doesn't know, go to another tea merchant.

Does your merchant or catalogue source list a name not found in this book? Does something from this list intrigue you but it's not in your merchant's catalogue? It is quite likely that the tea may be listed by other names. It could also be that the tea is one made in limited quantities, but your tea merchant might be able to find it for you. That's what the pleasure of green tea is all about—hunting down those favourites.

A GUIDE TO CHINESE TEAS

The encyclopedia of Chinese teas, *Zhongguo Chajing*, lists 138 distinct green teas, of which there are more than 12,500 subgroups—often duplications, imitations and lower or higher grades of the same kinds of teas.

CHINA TEAS (CHA)

The best green teas are thought to be those picked in early spring at the time of the Qing Ming festival, always 5 April of the solar calendar. Tribute teas are those exceptional spring teas chosen to be presented to emperors long ago and now given to high officials or honoured guests of the government. Those leaves harvested from June to December are thought to create the better oolongs because the more mature leaves have a greater solids content and may be oxidised longer to acquire that special oolong 'finish'.

Most modern tea masters list 500 or more green teas, and everyone agrees that there are many more, some of which are never exported because they are grown in such small quantities. In addition to these dizzying statistics, teas can vary from one farm to the next in the same region; they could be given different names from plucking to plucking, processed slightly differently, and, of course, may taste slightly different. Instead of viewing this as frustrating, most tea lovers find it still another reason to try the next cup and the next, always hoping for the holy grail of tea, the perfect cup. It's intoxicating, it's exciting—it is the romance of tea.

Pouchong
Pouchong (or wrapped tea) is an 'in between' tea. Not truly a green, it is also not wholly an oolong. I confess to including several pouchongs because they are personal favourites. The other reason is that many tea sellers include them in their lists of greens.

Pouchongs are oxidised in a unique way. They are wrapped in cloth or paper to keep the leaves moist longer during the heat-generated oxidation; the result is that most pouchongs are oxidised 12–18 per cent. In contrast, greens are not oxidised at all, oolongs are oxidised from 1–80 per cent, and blacks are oxidised 100 per cent.

The following teas are typically available in most serious tea shops, mail-order catalogues and on-line sources operated by merchants dedicated to a good general inventory of green teas.

GREEN TEA

AFTER THE SNOW SPROUTING
Long silvery buds with a fresh green scent, these are among the first tender sprouts available after the winter snows, hence their eponymous name. This tea is delicate and lovely.

BAOZHONG (POUCHONG)
These are the tea leaves used most often as a base for jasmine because of the large, flavourful leaves and slightly longer oxidation, which holds the scent of the night-blooming jasmine so well.

CHING CHA (OR QING CHA)
Chinese for green tea grown in mainland China, of which there are basically three types: mei, or twisted; pearl, or rolled leaves; and ming cha or famous teas, which include such superior teas as Pi Lo Chun and Tai Ping Hou Gui.

CHUNMEE (PRECIOUS EYEBROWS)
Also spelled Chun Mei or Zhen Mei, the name is given to these good springtime greens because the leaves are twisted into small, curved shapes—not unlike the eyebrows on a beautiful doll. A high-grown tea from Yunnan province, it produces a remarkable aftertaste from its light amber infusion, reminiscent of plums. Multiple infusions are quite common from this subtle yet provocative tea. Some Chunmee has been grown in Zhejiang. Brew lightly, as it is easily overbrewed.

CURLED SILVER DRAGON
A complex, wonderful flavour with slightly sweet overtones is derived from thick, twisted, downy leaves of green and white.

DONG YANG DONG HAI
A Zhejiang green known for its flowery aroma and long-lasting taste—smooth, rich, and sweet—Dong Yang Dong Hai comes from high-grade yellow-green fairly open leaves and bud sets that give a mellow-tasting, medium body liquor.

CHINA TEAS (CHA)

DRAGONWELL (LONG JING OR LUNG CHING)

From Hangzhou in Zhejiang province comes the favourite green tea of mainland China. Its fresh, sweet taste has inspired poetry from Lu Yu's time to today. Its leaves are flat, long and vibrant green and will yield several infusions of delicate, flowery aroma and flavour from its yellow-green liquor.

Up to eight spring grades of Dragonwell are possible, with the highest grade usually designated as Qing Ming, as it is picked during the special spring festival when the finest tribute teas are picked. The tea must be picked during a narrow window of time marked by the festival, yet prior to the predictable spring rains. Should this tea be picked after the rain, no good tea will result.

The other grades of Dragonwell are extra special, special, and grades one to five. Each grade is different—sometimes slightly, sometimes radically—although each has that distinctive Dragonwell taste. The most important aspect of the top Dragonwells, however, is the appearance of buds; the second tier of quality has fine leaves but no buds, and the lowest tier of quality has only older leaves.

The four important qualities many teamen look for in Dragonwells are *se* (colour—jade green in the dry leaf), *xiang* (aroma), *wei* (taste), and *xing* (shape—flat, elegant leaves). Dragonwells are grown all over the Zhejiang province, and Lion's Peak Long Jing from the Tiemu Mountains is considered by many to be a premier grade.

This again brings up the critical point that your tea merchant should be able to identify his or her teas by grade, and in which area they are grown. Ask if the tea was cupped, and if he or she can describe the flavour points to you.

And, yes, there really is a dragon's well, located near West Lake in Zhejiang province and the village home of this tea. The dragon is the king of water in Chinese mythology. One legend explains that a drought came to the dragon's well monastery about AD 250, causing great hardship to the farming monks. One monk prayed specifically to the dragon, pleading for rain. Instantly, he was blessed with a steady downpour, and the monks once again had the water they needed to pursue their farming.

GREEN TEA

EMERALD TIPS
This is a Dragonwell 'type' of tea, grown near the famous area but not of the same quality. It is, nonetheless, a lovely, fragrant, complexly flavoured tea.

ESHAN PEKOE
From long and twisted leaves comes what is for some people an everyday tea; for others, its strong flavour is reserved only for special occasions. The tea is named for Eshan, a rough five-hour ride west of Kumming in Yunnan province.

GREEN PEARLS (SILK BALLS)
Rolled 'pearls' unfurl into three or four leaves that include a delicately pale tea-leaf bud. These pearls, also called balls or pellets, yield a lovely aromatic brew of a golden liquor with at least three to seven infusions. These are delightful to prepare for people new to green teas. The 'dance of the leaf' is spectacular, and the ensuing drink always satisfying. Some smaller pearls are infused with jasmine flowers, but the plain ones, typically the size of a 6mm pearl, are definitely fragrant without the additional scent of a flower.

GUNPOWDER
This is a tea shaped to look like small pellets that imitate the gunpowder pellets used for ammunition during the seventeenth century. It was one of the first teas ever to be exported from China to Europe and, as a result, remains one of the best known here. The original idea for rolling the leaves into tight balls or pellets was to help preserve their freshness for the long trip from China to Europe. The pellets are still lightly rolled combinations of buds and young green leaves. They unfurl as they infuse, offering a visual explanation for the 'agony of the leaves', the process so dramatically named in which the curled or rolled dried leaves are infused with water and open up 'agonisingly'.

Originally hand-rolled, most gunpowders are rolled by machine today. To test the freshness of gunpowder, pinch or squeeze a pellet in your hand. It should resist pressure if it's fresh; it will crumble if it's stale. However, as always, the truest test of freshness and goodness is to cup the tea, to drink it properly brewed, and let your palate be the final arbiter.

Gunpowder is frequently used in a tea blend for Moroccan mint, which incorporates a sweet digestive—the native Moroccan spearmint—with the clean, crisp taste of gunpowder green tea (see chapter 12).

Gunpowders are most commonly from Zhejiang province, and many come from other provinces, like Qinghai, Anhui, Hunan and Fujian, in a variety of grades. They brew up a dark liquor.

Gunpowder (Xiao Qiu). This type of gunpowder brews dark green with a pungent but pleasant flavour and long-lasting aftertaste. It lends itself well to added flavours like lemon or mint.

Gunpowder Temple of Heaven. A premier gunpowder from Zhejiang province, it provides an aromatic cup with a sweet grassy taste, much more delicate than the other grades.

Gunpowder Pinhead Temple of Heaven. This is similar to Gunpowder Temple of Heaven, but usually smaller. Considered a premier gunpowder type, it is quite common to elicit multiple infusions.

GUYUJIAN

Very mild-tasting delicate tea with pale green liquor, Guyujian looks not unlike the mist that covers the Yellow Mountains of Anhui province where it grows.

GUZHANG MAOHAN (MAO JIN)

A springtime sweet tea, harvested only during a ten-day period, the leaves of this tea are from bushes in the Yellow Mountains of Anhui province. They are dried into crinkly leaves with silver tips that provide a darker-coloured brew with a smooth, smoky flavour.

HYSON

In the eighteenth and nineteenth centuries, Hyson was sometimes associated with gunpowder teas, and was used frequently to describe tea in poems, along with 'bohea' (for oolong). Today, using the term 'Hyson' to describe Chinese teas is considered archaic. Still, some merchants carry teas named Hyson, and in several grades. India also has a green called Hyson, so it is best to ask your tea merchant whether the Hyson you are buying is Chinese or Indian. The Chinese Hysons are usually tightly twisted, and offer a rather surprisingly full-bodied liquor and many infusions. It is quite an enjoyable tea.

JASMINE

The jasmine flower, thought to have arrived in China from Persia, has been used to scent green teas for nearly ten centuries, at least since the Sung dynasty (AD 960–1279). The jasmine is unique among flowers blended with tea because it opens up only at night. As a result, scenting tea with jasmine is also done at night, by covering a bamboo tray or screen of fresh green tea leaves with a blanket of buds or flowers.

This is done in several layers, and in the morning the flowers are removed. This process is repeated, often up to eleven times, before the delicate fragrance becomes a part of the tea itself. The quality of both the green tea and the jasmine differentiates each of the following styles of jasmine teas. Those from Fujian province are considered to be the best. The following is a partial list.

Jasmine Chun Feng (Spring Peak Jasmine). With a wonderful aroma, this harvest green tea is a Chinese classic of uniform-size leaves with large amounts of silver tips. The uniformity reflects careful sorting and grading. A minimum of three infusions is common.

Jasmine Hummingbird's Nest. Considered a showplace tea, this is an exquisite jasmine that is pressed and rolled to form a little 'nest' and carefully protected with delicate paper folded in tight pleats. The paper is unwrapped, and the nest is placed in a tumbler or wine-glass and infused gently with water, about 66°C (150°F). It will then blossom out into leaves and proffer its most exquisite jasmine scent. This is a great way to enchant guests.

Jasmine Monkey King. A classic green tea with the divine jasmine scent marvellous for afternoon tea, this is an excellent marriage of good Chinese green tea and a lovely fragrance.

Jasmine Pearl. This tea is scented with the buds of the jasmine flower to create a very intense and fragrant tea. The leaves and the buds are rolled into small balls or pearls that unfurl as they are steeped, showing off their beautiful, graceful leaves. It will yield six or seven infusions. (A similar grade is sometimes referred to as Dragon Phoenix.)

Jasmine Yin Hao Silver Tip. Also called Fragrant Petal, this provides multiple infusions that do not fade in flavour. Its lingering aftertaste is superb. Often made with the strong-flavoured pouchong teas and allowed to oxidise slightly longer than most green teas, this jasmine is infinitely more aromatic than others in this category. Although pouchong tea is technically an oolong, a good grade is closer in taste to the great greens. A fine pouchong brews a pale green that is light, delicate, and without the 'fired' taste typical of most oolongs.

LU'AN MELON SEEDS (LUAN GUA PIAN)

Partly opened leaves that appear just to have been plucked and dried produce a pure, sweet flavour that does indeed evoke the summer sweetness of melon. Its leaves are strikingly green.

LU SHAN YUN WU (CLOUDS AND MIST)

One of the ten famous teas, this one is from the Jiangxi province, home to the Lu Mountains. It produces a clean, clear liquor with a refreshing taste.

MINMEI (FUJIAN EYEBROW)

Min is an old Chinese name for Fujian; mei means eyebrow. Minmei is an eyebrow tea that looks quite like a Pi Lo Chun, but is grown in the Fujian province. It is stronger tasting than Pi Lo Chun, and an economical tea to buy for all its flavour notes.

GREEN TEA

MOUNT EMEI HAIRPOINT
This is an exquisite, delicate tea made from downy leaves grown near the famous Mount Emei in Sichuan. Mount Emei is one of the five holy mountains known to be a stop for pilgrimages of Buddhist devotees who make the trip up to the famous Indian-styled temple via cable car, then climb several hundred steps to reach the temple and the Indian elephant sculpture nearby.

OSMANTHUS
One of the famous Chinese gui hua (orange blossoms), osmanthus is used to scent pouchong tea. It is quite subtle and incredible to drink alone or as a dessert tea.

PAI YUN (AKA BAI YUN OR WHITE CLOUD IMPERIAL)
A slightly curled, long, whitish leaf produces a very pale celadon liquor with a distinctive chestnutlike flavour.

PAN LONG YIN HAO
From Zhejiang province, this tea had a variegated leaf that produces a complex brew of multiple flavour notes. It has been a repeat winner in tea competitions conducted by China's ministry of agriculture. Whenever you find this particular tea, grab it.

PI LO CHUN
One of the famous ming cha teas, its old name, Astounding Fragrance, somehow seems more appropriate, which indeed it is. Today, however, it has been commonly translated as Green Snail Spring, Spiral Green Jade, or Silver Spiral Green.

This is an interesting tea, with small, twisted, curved leaves. It is produced in the early spring, and the delicacy of the season is quite evident in this premier tea. It produces a slightly sweet, velvety yellowish liquor whose aftertaste is lovely.

In mainland China, Pi Lo Chun is grown in the Dong Ding Mountains of Suzhou and has overtones of fruit trees that grow nearby. The Taiwanese version of Pi Lo Chun is ultra-fragrant and quite wonderful, but its leaves are shaped completely differently.

CHINA TEAS (CHA)

SNOW DRAGON
Near the border between Fujian province and south-east Zhejiang province are the bushes that produce this beautiful tea. Its hand-fashioned leaves are elegant and flat, and every step of the process is done by hand. It is roasted in a large wok to produce a leaf that brings you a nutty, sweet flavour in the cup.

SPARROW'S TONGUE
A Dragonwell 'look-alike', this tea is actually from the Sichuan province, and provides a pale, yellowish liquor with a sweet green flavour and a fragrance that is wonderful, wonderful, wonderful.

TAIPING HOUGUI
Its very long leaves are from bushes grown in the Anhui province. They give multiple infusions of a mild liquor with fruity overtones that some recall as orchid, although it is not scented with orchids.

TIANMU MOUNTAIN
To serve this tea, wash the leaves by pouring water on them for thirty seconds; discard the liquor. Add water and infuse for two minutes. This brings out the full flavour of this very complex tea with a definite astringency that satisfies but does not overpower.

TIANMU QING TING
A delicate green tea with matching aroma and pleasant feel in the mouth, this is a treat for the entire olfactory system.

YU HUA (RAIN FLOWER)
Long, elegant, pointed leaves give a fresh tasting liquor in the cup, similar to the complexity of a Pi Lo Chun but more delicate.

YUNNAN GREEN NEEDLE
This subtle tea with a pleasant astringency is made from uniform, delicate green buds with pointed tips that give a clean-tasting liquor.

GREEN TEA

Chinese showplace teas

These speciality teas come in hundreds of different sizes and shapes, and are made with an enormous variety of teas. The fun is to astonish your guests by placing these teas in a glass tumbler or wine-glass, infusing with rather cool water (150°F; 66°C), and watching them 'blossom' into their particular shapes for marvellous table-top drama. And they taste good, too.

Here is just a sampling to whet your appetite. Your tea merchant has many more, which may be referred to as rosettes, mudans, sea anemones, or peonies. They may also be named either for the fruit or object that the infused leaves 'become' or for the shape the dried leaves form, such as plum, ball or strawberry.

GREEN CHRYSANTHEMUM (OR GREEN PEONY)
A green tea from Fujian province, its leaves are tied together into a flattened bundle, sometimes referred to as a rosette. When infused, it has the shape, if not the colour, of a chrysanthemum.

GREEN LYCHEE
Green tea leaves are tied in a bundle at their base rather than their middle. The leaves are then folded back onto themselves and develop a unique round shape like the lychee fruit. When brewed, the leaves blossom and get fuller.

GREEN PLUM (OR SPRING PLUM)
The tips of the thick green leaves are cut off to form a flat disk, about the size of a five pence piece. When infused, it forms the shape of a plum or ball. Leaves are from Fujian province.

GREEN TUO CHA (GREEN BOWL TEA)
A form of brick tea made from green leaves but quite small, the pressed leaves are shaped into a small round 'bowl' with a slight depression in the middle. It looks similar to the Jasmine Hummingbird's Nest but is unscented. This tea offers several cups of a delicate mellow flavour with definite smoky undertones, evoking the signature quality of teas from Yunnan province.

CHAPTER 5

Indian Teas (Chai)

*In Assam dwelt her ancient family,
And there ... grew graceful India tea.*
E. M. Ford, 'A Tea Idyl' from
The Tea and Coffee Journal (1909)

Nestling in the Himalayas, and braced against the Blue Mountains or lining the rolling plains along the Brahmaputra River, Indian teas bathe in the mist of early morning. Combined with a magical combination of altitude, weather and a dedication to cultivating this remarkable plant, India has become the largest producer of teas in the world.

Indian teas are processed in all categories: black, oolong, white, and the light and lovely greens. They all retain the essence, character and integrity of the three major regions: Darjeeling, Nilgiri and Assam.

Distinct aroma and appearance

India teas have generally longer and wider leaves than Chinese teas. The slight processing green teas undergo will still showcase the intrinsic taste characteristics reflected in the three major regions of tea growing in India: Nilgiri, the fragrant one; Assam, the hearty one; and Darjeeling, the delicate one. Indian greens are slightly astringent, have a crisp bite, and are less delicate than Chinese greens. All are excellent paired with foods.

Processing makes the difference
The processing of teas in India is quite mechanised and industrialised, and green teas are no exception. Green tea production remains

limited, however, because completely separate machinery must be dedicated only to green tea processing so that neither black nor oolong teas ever contaminate the tea or the machines. If the same machinery is used for all three processes, it will ruin the taste of the teas.

Today there is a core of dedicated green tea processors, largely on organic farms, and most use machinery to air-dry and roll the leaves and sort them into various sizes and grades. It is simply too expensive to match the elaborate hand-withering and hand-rolling techniques that China uses for much of its classic green teas.

Growth of organic teas

One very exciting trend is the interest in organic farming, especially on tea estates. As with all change, there are a number of hurdles to overcome. For example, organic methods are definitely being used on some estates, but on land that has absorbed pesticides for decades. These pesticides don't simply go away the moment the farmer decides not to use them any more, and a considerable investment of time and money must be made by those dedicated enough to the principles of organic farming.

The ideal situation is to allow the earth to lie fallow, rest, regenerate and be nourished with health-giving nutrients prior to beginning an organic farming programme. Some farmers simply cannot afford this; they must seek other sources of income as they wait for their farms to regenerate. As you can imagine, this can lower the farmer's incentive to go organic.

Should a farmer dedicate a part of his farm to organic tea bushes, he must also consider all the crops around the tea farm; they too must be organically grown, or by osmosis, symbiosis, and other phenomena in the soil his originally dedicated organic tea bushes will be contaminated by all those other tea bushes or crops grown nearby.

Organic farming takes a lot of manpower, not only for planting and harvesting but also for processing—particularly in creating green teas in a country where more than 85 per cent of the teas are processed as black teas. Before they invest the considerable sums of money that are required to buy new machinery dedicated solely to processing green tea and to train the many tea processors and tasters needed, organic farmers in India need to know they have a substantial, reliable market.

The severest standards for organic produce of any kind exist in the state of California and in Japan and Germany. If your organic teas meet these standards, you do indeed have a quality organic product.

Pioneering organic farmers

Two Indian tea farms that can unequivocally be called organic are the Oothu Tea Estate, the first organic green tea farm in the world, and Makaibari Tea Estates, the first truly biodynamically grown organic tea producer in the world.

Oothu lies in 312 hectares in southern India and cultivates teas without any artificial pesticides or chemicals. The largest estate of organically cultivated tea in the world, it produces more than one million kilograms per year of both green and black tea, and has cultivated them strictly organically since 1988.

Using oil seed cake as a benign fertiliser, the Oothu Tea Estate farmers have seen great improvement in soil conditions and conservation. Nature's own way of soil enrichment—vermiculture, in which the earth is improved in stages—is also used. To complete the cycle, the entire processing of the tea is done organically and simply to produce a superior green tea.

Makaibari Tea Estates is not only 100 per cent organic, but also the world's first biodynamically cultivated tea garden. It follows the principles of Rudolf Steiner, who created a concept in 1924 of a community living in harmony with nature, emphasising organic, sustainable methods of cultivation.

Makaibari produces an authentic, unblended Darjeeling tea without any artificial ingredients. Managed by the great-grandson of the founder, who established the garden in 1859, it covers 1,575 acres of forest, valleys and hills. Nearly 1,000 acres have been preserved as a subtropical forest with an enormous variety of vegetation and foliage and many species of wildlife, from leopards and panthers to deer, boars and wild Himalayan mountain goats.

Makaibari's workers live, work and raise their children on the estate, which offers them free child care, allows no child labour and guarantees employment to children of retired workers. Management helps the workers maintain vegetable gardens and raise farm and dairy animals, and even teaches them how to generate biogas as a renewable, nonpolluting cooking fuel.

Owner Swaraj Kumar 'Rajah' Banerjee feels that drinking a high-quality Darjeeling like Makaibari is like 'drinking the spirit of the estate where everyone is involved, and everyone has contributed'.

A GUIDE TO INDIAN TEAS

Green teas are a rather small part of the overall production in India, but as green tea continues to make headlines as a health-giving beverage, the market may widen, with more estates turning over part of their crops and, more importantly, part of their processing budgets to make even better green teas. In the meantime, whenever you buy a green tea you like, buy it again. Your money is the only way to encourage the industry.

ASSAM

India's most plentiful tea district, Assam covers about 200 tea gardens that produce up to one-third of all the tea of India. The area is located along the borders of China, Burma and Bangladesh, about 125 miles east of the area of Darjeeling. In the nineteenth century, as we have seen, the Scottish Major Robert Bruce 'discovered' the *Thea assamica* on the high plateau along the banks of the Brahmaputra River. Thus began the modern history of growing tea in India. The Assam tea bush has larger, wider leaves, but is only slightly different from the Chinese tea bush, *Camellia sinensis*. Assam teas are grown for 'strength' in aroma and body, and only a tiny part is processed as green teas. Not surprisingly, these greens have a hearty taste and are quite favoured by those new to the taste of green tea.

INDIAN TEAS (CHAI)

Bherjan Estate. An organic green tea estate, Bherjan's crop produces small, dark leaves that infuse to a very pleasant, light tasting green tea. This is an excellent everyday, all-day tea.

Kohngea. The green version of this tea is clean tasting and gives several crisp infusions of delicate green liquor.

DARJEELING

Some 86 gardens grow tea in Darjeeling, the district on the southern hills of the Himalayas along the border with Nepal, Sikkim and Bhutan. Darjeelings, often referred to as the champagne of teas, are among the most sought after for their tender, highly aromatic leaves from the first flush of spring, and for the more flowery teas of the autumnal picking. Here, as elsewhere in India, green tea processing is very limited, but the teas are exquisite—delicate yet with that distinctive Darjeeling astringency that is so admired.

Caveat emptor: As with all Darjeelings, try to buy single-estate green teas only. It is a truism in the tea business that more Darjeeling is sold than could ever be manufactured; each year, 11 million kilos are grown, but more than 50 million kilos are reported sold! People blend it with other things (which is fine) but call it Darjeeling (which is not fine). A blend can produce a good cup of tea, but should definitely be called a blend and not passed off as being only one type of tea.

Ambootia Tea Estate. This estate grows several grades of green that produce a light, lovely cup. Its teas are frequently found in many commercial brands of organic greens.

Arya Green. An aromatic, gentle green from Darjeeling, this tea is equivalent in looks and style to a Japanese sencha but with much more flavour.

Makaibari Tea Estates. This tea estate produces a biodynamically grown world-class tea with elegant, long, full leaves that infuse several times. A multiple-award winner, the tea offers the essence of Darjeeling and the lightness of a green. Add to that the care and integrity of an organic leaf, and you have an enormously satisfying cup.

GREEN TEA

Risheehat Estate. A Darjeeling green produced from a limited crop, this is sought after for its fruity aroma and mild, delicate, sweet taste. It yields a lovely fragrance and clear green-yellow liquor.

Seeyok (Swek Chiyakaman). Located on the Indo-Nepal border facing Rongbong Valley, Seeyok produces a green with the classic organic Darjeeling character.

Semabeong (Abode of the Bear). Located at perhaps the highest altitude in Darjeeling, this tea garden was only recently revived and produces an interesting organic green tea.

NILGIRI

Unlike Darjeeling or Assam, the teas in Nilgiri grow all year long, producing an extremely aromatic tea that is ideal for blending with fruit or flower essences or with other teas. It is in the south of India among the spectacular range of the Nilgiris, the Blue Mountains, and its teas are often referred to as 'the fragrant ones'. Although the production of greens is limited, as elsewhere in India, Nilgiri greens retain their famous scent and offer an interesting cup.

Craigmore Estate. This Nilgiri tea estate provides a limited amount of green that has high-grown flavour and a matching sweet taste, reflecting its high elevation of growth (the highest in Nilgiri). It is a very accessible and enjoyable tea.

Nilgiri Green. This tea from Nilgiri (Tamil for 'blue mountains') is intoxicating in its aroma. The taste is gentle and clean—excellent to drink all day long.

Oothu. A very satisfying green from pretty, flat, elegant leaves.

OTHER INDIA GREENS

Chunmee. This is not an area but a type of Indian green tea, similar to the 'eyebrow' tea of China, made more like a loosely rolled gunpowder. It is very pleasant, with the essence of India teas in the cup, and can be made from any type of green tea.

Hyson. This is not an area, but a grade of green tea that cups a pleasant, lively brew.

INDIAN TEAS (CHAI)

Kangra. A small tea-growing region in the northern state of Himachai Pradesh. For decades Kangra has produced green teas—primarily a popular rolled tea resembling gunpowder pellets—for its neighbours in Afghanistan.

CHAPTER 6

Japanese Teas (O-cha)

When tea is made with water drawn from the depths of mind
Whose bottom is beyond measure,
We really have what is called cha-no-yu.
                    A verse given to Sen-no Rikyu
                    by his shogun, Toyotomi Hideyoshi

Although it is usually ranked sixth to eighth among the largest producers of tea in the world, Japan consumes nearly all that it produces. Most is grown in the Shizuoka region, but other important areas include Miye, Kagoshima, Kyoto (Uji), Nara, and Saitama. Rich in vitamin C, Japanese green teas are also low in theophylline (a stimulant) and excellent alone or with meals.

Distinct aroma and appearance

Japanese teas range from the earthy brown of a roasted green like bancha, usually made from the older, more brittle leaves, to the exquisite deep hue of their finest green tea, known as gyokuro (Precious Dew).

The most common green in Japan is sencha, a vivid green tea with smooth leaves that provides a clear yellow-green liquor. Spiderleg is a long, elegantly twisted green that makes a rich cup, and the highest quality green, gyokuro, is short, thick, and intensely green with leaves that proffer a remarkable, almost ephemeral taste. These three, the most popular greens of Japan, are made in a pristine way—free of stems or twigs—and are beautiful, with a pure tea flavour.

The twig teas are earthy low grades made not from leaves but from twigs and stems. They are smooth-tasting because of the expert roasting process used.

Processing makes the difference

Most Japanese green teas are made from beautifully handled leaves, and much of their elegance and rich colour is due to their style of processing: steaming immediately after plucking, then air-drying. This two-step process does much to preserve the flavour, the fragrance and the beautiful colour of the teas, particularly gyokuro but also sencha, the everyday green tea of Japan.

Processing gyokuro
Japanese greens, especially gyokuro, are vivid hunter green. Their colour is enhanced by covering the bushes with black cloth or bamboo curtains to shield them from the sunlight and help the leaves produce more chlorophyll. Gyokuro is usually steamed by machine and heated in a drying machine, then the stalks are removed by finishing tools. To achieve the elegant pine-needle shapes, gyokuro is rolled and twisted.

Processing matcha
The finest matcha is made from gyokuro. When processing matcha, the rolling and twisting steps typical of the gyokuro process are skipped. Instead, the leaves go directly to a stone grinder, which pulverises the leaves into a silky chartreuse powder. The powdery texture is critical to making the frothy tea of the chanoyu.

Processing bancha and sencha
Those Japanese teas grown on an open plantation, like bancha or sencha, are steamed, rolled and twisted by machine before they are put into drying machines. Next comes an automated selector, which sorts the teas before the finishing tools remove the stalks and debris. Hojicha and other 'roasted' teas undergo the additional step of pan-roasting to achieve a mild, nutty taste.

GREEN TEA

A GUIDE TO JAPANESE TEAS

In comparison with the two major giants in tea, India and China, Japan produces a remarkably large amount given its excruciatingly small area. The prefectures of Shizuoka and Uji provide the best quality teas, but exports are minimal compared to other tea-producing countries because of the massive home consumption—especially of the high-quality greens.

BANCHA (LATE HARVEST)

Low on the tea totem pole, this is ordinary, dark, and rough. Mixed with stems, stalks, and low-grade teas, it is the everyday drink of Japan. Bancha has a slightly astringent taste and produces a yellowish liquor. Green bancha is bitter when cool. To brew it, use three rounded tablespoons of bancha leaves to a pot of three cups of boiling water. Let steep two or three minutes and pour into warmed cups. Do not allow the leaves to continue to steep; pour off all the tea at once. For a single cup, use about a level teaspoon in 165ml (6fl oz) of hot water (82°C, 180°F) and steep about two minutes. Bancha may be re-infused, and is frequently served along with sake.

FUKUIJYU

The rich, mouth-full taste is an important aspect of this pan-fired green with the shiny green leaves. Its pale liquor belies a lingering taste.

GENMAICHA

This tea is a mixture of bancha or medium quality green tea, popped corn and toasted, hulled rice kernels. This is a nutty, simple drink that tastes quite wonderful with typical Japanese foods. It is not a fine tea in any sense of the word, but an inexpensive, everyday tea drink that is fun, full of flavour and satisfying. Brew one teaspoon in 165ml (6fl oz) of 82°C (180°F) water for about 1½ minutes.

JAPANESE TEAS (O-CHA)

GYOKURO (GEM OF DEW DROP, JEWEL DEW, OR PRECIOUS DEW)
This is a premier, noble green tea made from single buds that are picked but once a year, resulting in a smaller crop. In an effort to develop increased chlorophyll, the tea garden is covered with black curtains, or with bamboo or straw shades, for three weeks in early spring. Leaves are picked about two weeks after they are covered. The leaves are small—about 2cm (¾in) long—and extremely fragrant and tender. Carefully prepared by light steaming, the dark green leaves produce a smooth, light-green liquor. Gyokuro has been referred to as 'history, philosophy and art in a single cup'. This is the best green tea of Japan; dried and powdered, it is the base for the matcha tea of the chanoyu. Usually brewed in a kyusu and served in handleless cups, gyokuro should be made with about one level teaspoon of long, thin leaves in about 120ml (4fl oz) water at 49°C (120°F). Steeped for about 1½ minutes, the tea is poured off completely. The leaves can be re-infused with slightly hotter water.

HOUJICHA
This tea drink is a bancha that is lightly roasted, which gives it a nutty flavour. Not at all a connoisseur tea, but a fun everyday drink that goes well with Japanese foods, particularly sukiyaki or any food strongly flavoured with soy sauce. Its liquor is a tawny brownish colour with a smoky taste. Although best when served hot, it can also be served cool but not cold. It is excellent at night-time, as it is very light and low in caffeine.

KOKEICHA
This tea is made from a paste of matcha and water, which is poured through tiny holes in boards or cardboard to become thin strings. When dried, the strings are cut into pieces of about 6mm (¼in), and brewed in hot water (82°C, 180°F) for several minutes. Sometimes referred to as 'spaghetti tea', it has a nice nutty overtone and pale yellow infused liquor.

GREEN TEA

KUKICHA
An everyday tea made from the twigs or stems of the tea bush. Makes a mild tea that is favoured by children and elderly people.

MATCHA UJI (FROTH OF LIQUID JADE)
This is the famous powdered green tea made by pulverising the highest quality gyokuro tea into a fine powder the consistency of talc. The steamed leaves are dried flat and mechanically ground. In centuries past, leaves were ground by hand with a mortar and pestle.

Matcha is used primarily in chanoyu. It is made by pouring hot water (about 85°C, 185°F) onto the powdered tea in a warmed small bowl rather than a teapot. A dampened bamboo whisk is used to stir up the matcha and water into a frothy drink that is at once sweet and astringent. Use about ½ teaspoon tea to 50ml water for thin tea, or two level teaspoons to 120ml water for thick tea.

Some people find it bitter, but the frothier the mix the less astringent it is. Japanese bean cakes—dried confectionery called *higashi*—or traditional sweets are used in the tea ceremony. A sweet biscuit will help offset any bitterness you discover. Served in a tea bowl, matcha is usually drunk from the bowl in three long sips followed by a pause. This pattern is continued until the portion is consumed.

Matcha is also made from lesser grades of green teas, which means lots of caffeine. Hiki-cha is a powdered green tea with very coarse grains; it is not used in chanoyu.

CRYO KUCHA (O'CHA CRYOKUCHA)
This common Japanese tea is not processed with any great flair.

SENCHA (INFUSED TEA)
Hunter green, needlelike leaves mark the sencha, which brews up to a delicate green liquor that is both grassy sweet and cleanly astringent. The grades are numerous, and even the mediocre sencha can be a delight—but if you can afford the better ones, be prepared for a treat. Many Pan-Asian countries are now processing greens

JAPANESE TEAS (O-CHA)

to imitate Japanese sencha and to meet the growing demand worldwide. China and Vietnam both make senchas, although most are exported to Japan.

Sencha is referred to as a 'guest tea' because it is of higher quality than, say, bancha or houjicha. Usually it is prepared with great ceremony in a special small teapot with its spout at '9 o'clock' and handle at '6 o'clock' instead of opposite one another. Called *kyusu*, the pots are used with small handleless cups made of porcelain. Sencha is excellent with sushi.

To brew, warm a small kyusu with hot water and empty it. Place two rounded teaspoons of sencha leaves in the pot and add about 230ml of hot water (80°C, 175°F), Steep for just one minute and pour a little tea into each warmed cup. Repeat until the cups are filled. In this way each guest receives the same quality and amount of tea. Completely pour off the liquor. Sencha is particularly rich in vitamin C, and may be infused several times.

Sencha Rose. This is a traditional sencha scented or flavoured with the essence of roses—quite a melange of aromatic and taste sensations.

Sencha Sakuro. Drinking this tea is like capturing springtime in Japan. It is a sencha green tea scented with the country's famous cherry blossoms. Some commercial brands use maraschino cherries.

SPIDERLEG

One of the most elegant greens, this tea comes in a variety of shapes, but look for long twisted leaves—spider legs—that, when brewed, open up to a beautiful green. Spiderleg is light tasting and exquisite in flavour.

SPIDERLEG SAKURO

This is scented and similar to Sencha Sakuro, but the leaves are longer and more 'spidery' than sencha leaves. The twisted leaves, when infused, produce a rich bouquet and lots of flavour, and the cherry scent is a lovely addition.

CHAPTER 7

Other Sources of Green Tea

In the taste of a single cup of tea you will eventually discover the truth of all the ten thousand forms in the universe. It is difficult to put this taste into words or to even catch a hint of it.
—The Venerable Ch'an (Zen) Master Kyongbong Sunim, in John Blofield's *The Chinese Art of Tea* (1985)

India, China and Sri Lanka are the world's largest producers of tea out of more than thirty-five tea-producing countries. Sri Lanka, formerly known as Ceylon, produces millions of kilos of black teas, and is emerging as a secondary green tea market to watch.

Although green tea has always been the tea of choice drunk every day in many Pan-Asian countries, it is used generally without much ceremony or elaborate techniques, and is of lower quality than that produced by the 'big three'. Vietnam, Malaysia and Indonesia, for example, grow their own tea but quantities are minuscule in comparison. We can only hope that as the demand for tea, particularly green tea, drives the marketplace, the quality and attention to tea production will also increase.

INDONESIA

Like much of Asia, Indonesia produces a great deal of green tea—the everyday tea of its people—and exports to neighbouring countries. Among Indonesian green teas found in the West are the fragrant Jasmine and the rolled green teas Gunpowder and Chunmee, which are made in the style of Chinese gunpowders and chunmees, and are graded.

OTHER SOURCES OF GREEN TEA

KOREA (CH'A)

Unlike most Asian countries where green tea is the everyday drink, Korea grows a tiny amount (about 1,000 tons) and exports even less. Of the three teas I've tasted, each was remarkable for fragrance and flavour, and very expensive.

At first the monks drank a form of powdered tea that was cut off in pieces from tea bricks. Not until the modern Yi period (1392–1910) was green tea introduced, but it quickly became known for its ability to purify blood, increase appetite and resist sleep—an important component of meditation.

Korean teas are still grown primarily by monasteries as they have been for centuries, but the finest teas come from the Posŏng area which has the perfect combination of loamy soil, lots of rain and the right balance of shade and sun.

Korean green tea, nok'cha, is processed as leaf tea, powdered tea or ball tea (like Chinese pearls or gunpowder). The fresh leaves for Chung-ch'a, for example, are plunged just for a moment into nearly boiling water, drained for several hours, then dried over a fire. Drying and rolling are done at the same time over the heat for several hours, eliciting an intense fragrance.

Pucho'ch'a is dried in an iron pot over a wood fire or in a mechanised drier, stirred to prevent overdrying or burning, then removed from the heat and rubbed and rolled by gloved women, to curl the leaves into themselves. The leaves are then returned to the heat and the whole process is repeated several more times.

The Mudung-sa monks grow and harvest spring snow tea (chon sol) on the slopes adjacent to their temple. The small leaves are cut very early in their growth, steamed in the early morning dew and mist, and dried nine times rather than using intense heat or cold which the monks believe would spoil the delicate leaves.

The Korean tea ceremony is quite lovely and much more formal than that of China, with women servers trained in 'tea art'. Water is first boiled, then cooled, then briefly steeped with tea before being served in beautiful vessels. The tea is likely to be chonch'a

GREEN TEA

(thin tea leaves) or chomch'a (thin leaves ground into a powder), although hosts often use the elegant, freshly plucked and costly chaksol ch'a (sparrow's tongue tea) for special guests.

NEPAL

Because it is so close to the Indian province of Darjeeling, Nepal produces teas with the distinctive Darjeeling character—delicate yet fruity, with a spicy, biting aroma.

A Guide to Nepalese Green Teas

Nepal produces very little tea for the export market but a few are being introduced in some Western countries. They are modest in price, and good with spicy foods.

Arniko. A rough but pleasant-tasting green tea, Arniko is made from barely processed greens from the tea bushes growing in the high elevations of Nepal. This tea is named after one of Nepal's famous generals.

SRI LANKA (FORMERLY KNOWN AS CEYLON)

Sri Lanka, perhaps one of the most stunningly beautiful countries in the world, has been producing tea for more than 130 years. In 1867 Scotsman James Taylor first planted tea seedlings in the Hewaheta Lower District. Today, Sri Lanka's tea growers produce more than 600 million pounds of tea yearly, on more than 1,000 estates, many small farms, and a few giant plantations.

The finest Ceylon teas come from the high-grown areas of Kandy, Nuwara Eliya, Uva and Uva Highlands, which provide teas with remarkable fragrance and brisk taste. The medium- to high-grown varieties from Pettiagalla, Kenilworth and Dimbulla are popular as afternoon teas.

To a smaller degree, green tea is being produced on Kalupahan in Haldumulla District, Mahavilla in Newalapitiya, Elpitiya in Kandy, Gurukoya in Nuware Eliya, and Stony Cliff in Kotagala. Organic

OTHER SOURCES OF GREEN TEA

teas are also increasing, and Needwood and Indulgashena in Haputale are being exported.

A Guide to Sri Lankan Green Teas

Sri Lanka's everyday green tea has the same brightness and clean taste that make black Ceylons so enjoyable. While green tea production is limited, there is growing interest that may encourage increased production in the next decade. There are already a number of organic green teas available from such outstanding tea-growing provinces as Uva and Dimbulla. Look for the following estate names and companies for quality organic teas from Sri Lanka: John Keeks, Ltd., James Finlay JEDB, Stassens Export, Silver Land, Denzil Soza New Elpitiya, and Green Field Estate, operated by Lanka Organic, a well-certified and respected company.

Ceylon Green. This is a generic name given to a wide variety of greens made from Sri Lankan teas. Ask your tea merchant if he or she can identify the plantation.

Ceylon Green Uva. A lovely, clean high-grown tea from Sri Lanka's prestigious Uva district, this is the ideal tea for drinking all day long.

Ceylon Jasmine. A Ceylon green tea scented with jasmine, this is much less delicate than the Chinese or Formosa style, but still fragrant and interesting.

Cotaganga. This important plantation previously made greens but has ceased to do so. They may return to processing green tea in the very near future.

Mungra. This is a light-tasting green with leaves that literally puff up during the drying process. Sometimes referred to as puffed rice tea, it is definitely a green with a mild, light taste.

Ratnapura. A gunpowder green made from the brisk Ceylon tea leaves of this estate. It is refreshing and light tasting.

GREEN TEA

TAIWAN (FORMERLY KNOWN AS FORMOSA)

Many tea manufacturers in Taiwan are descendants of the famous tea growers who crossed the straits of Taiwan. They settled in Pinglin, now the site of the world's largest tea museum—a must-see for anyone interested in tea, its history, culture and accoutrements. Upon their arrival, they discovered that the lush, verdant land was remarkably similar to their homeland, and they began a long and productive tea-making tradition. Many still use the same ancient technique of drying tea leaves in the sun, creating a unique partial oxidation that results in a very distinctive, somewhat sweet 'Formosa' aroma and a very rich and complex taste.

This partial oxidation process is also used for an 'in-between' tea, the pouchong. Pouchong is a cross between the green and oolong, but most tea masters classify it as oolong. Pouchongs are frequently used in jasmines and other scented teas to mimic classic mainland China's scented teas, especially when a less sweet tea is desired.

A Guide to Taiwanese Teas

The following is just a partial list; the best Formosa greens have skyrocketed in price in recent years and many are still not available in great quantities, but when you find them, try them.

Formosa Gunpowder. Lots of body and bite, and an interesting alternative to traditional gunpowders; nicely wrapped leaves in the traditional pellet style. Infuses to a light, clear green.

Formosa Long Jing. Brighter green than mainland China Long Jings, this has a lot of white tips and produces a very gentle tea with lots of body and aroma, very little astringency, and a 'bright' flavour that is palate-cleansing and very pleasant.

Formosa Pouchong. This is technically an oolong but is sought after by green-tea lovers for its light and delicate taste that is reminiscent of fine greens. It offers more of a bite than mainland China green.

Green Oolong or Tung-Ting Oolong. This is another example of an in-between tea, one that is oxidised 18 per cent to retain a green character. It yields a sweet, aromatic cup typical of Taiwanese oolong, yet the leaves remain quite green. It provides a multilayered taste experience.

Jade Oolong. An innovative 'new' tea, Jade Oolong is very delicate, sweet, smooth, and quite generous—up to five infusions is quite common. It is a very relaxing and remarkable any-time-of-the-day tea. Although named 'oolong', its smooth, flat leaves are decidedly green and oxidised about 15 to 18 per cent to capture the best of both processes.

Pi Lo Chun. This is an excellent example of how the place where tea grows affects not only flavour, but appearance and style. True Pi Lo Chun is grown in Zhejiang in mainland China and produces a downy, curled leaf tea that is very delicate. The Pi Lo Chun from Taiwan, however, is a long twisted leaf without any down, and provides a nutty, fresh flavour and a pale celadon colour. Even though it is not a 'true' Pi Lo Chun, it is a tea that combines the smoothness, delicacy and heady aroma indicative of any premier tea.

VIETNAM (CHÈ OR TRÀ)

It is always surprising to note that Vietnam is one of the top ten producers of tea in a world of more than thirty-five tea-producing countries. True, Vietnam produces considerably less than the top three (India, China and Sri Lanka), but it is definitely a tea source to watch—especially for greens.

Some tea connoisseurs believe that Vietnam may be the actual birthplace of the world's second most popular beverage. Many ancient tea bushes still stand in the gentle valley on Vietnam's northern border with China.

The high-grown tea from Vietnam produces small leaves that make a sweet, lovely tea. The greens, the everyday teas of the Vietnamese people, are refreshing, sweetish, and give the typically clean taste that quality greens do.

Vietnamese teas are processed by a variety of methods, including the most traditional: steaming, pan-firing, and air-drying. With the latest influx of Hong Kong-based and Japanese investors, many processing plants now sport state-of-the-art machinery for the final processing. Still, one can find stalwarts who eschew the one-leaf-fits-all concept and still hand-process their teas.

A Guide to Vietnamese Green Teas

The following is just an inkling of what may come our way in the future.

Bác Thái. This everyday tea of Vietnam produces a yellow liquor that has a cooling effect on the body, a necessity in this humidity-drenched area. Grown in the northern mountain areas of Thái Nguyên province north of Hanoi, it is light, sweet, and really can be drunk all day. As with all teas, different grades produce different quality.

Bao Lôc. A fine green tea grown in the southern area of Vietnam commonly used to create jasmine and, sometimes, the precious Chè Sen (Lotus Tea), it is rarely seen outside Vietnam.

Chè Sen (Lotus Tea). This is the most famous tea from the central highlands of Vietnam. In the era of Emperor Tu Duc (1848–1883), his servants would prepare his lotus tea by collecting dew from the lotus leaves every morning. Its essence surrounds the temples and pagodas of Vietnam.

Today, Chè Sen is created with either a Bác Thái or Bao Lôc base and scented with the flowers and inner seeds of the exquisitely fragrant lotus blossom. During the evening, the lotus flower bud is carefully opened and a few grams of perfect Bác Thái or Bao Lôc tea leaves are inserted. Then the petals are gently closed. It is one of the most popular teas from Vietnam.

Hà Giang. A Shan tea grown organically along the Chinese border where the tea bushes are literally ancient, its leaves and buds are dark green and it produces a very complex yet well-balanced tea. Most buds are pale because they have not developed their full chlorophyll content; these buds are definitely green—quite an anomaly.

OTHER SOURCES OF GREEN TEA

Sencha. A 'look-alike' of the Japanese style of green tea, it is sweet and fresh and created generally for the Japanese market.

Shan. A common tea, it is processed both as a black, Trần Phú (Tuyêt), and as a green (Hà Giang).

CHAPTER 8

Buying, Storing and Brewing

Come, let us have some tea and continue to talk about happy things.
Chaim Potok, *The Chosen*

When purchasing green teas, please note that appearance and colour in themselves are not always the clues to the quality of the tea. Sometimes a tea can be nicely rolled but its taste is mediocre. Also, high-grade greens are sometimes more grey than green in their dried form.

Your tea merchant should really know his or her inventory and be able to answer questions about how old the tea is, how it was stored prior to delivery, and how it is stored in the shop. Properly stored teas can last for months, but the finest tea will lose its flavour profile in days if not properly stored.

Testing for freshness

Green tea is a beverage that is most readily enjoyed visually because of the delicate colour in its infused liquor. It is important that the tea be fresh, and the best way to test its freshness is to close your fist tightly round a small amount, breathe in with your nose, then release your fingers.

Smell the aroma that has been released from the tea. Is it sweet? Grassy? Pleasant? If there is no odour or a very faint aroma, the tea is most likely not fresh enough; discard it. Although this method will tell you much, nothing will reveal the true essence of the tea like cupping it—brewing it with the correct amounts of tea leaves and water heated to the right temperature, followed with the proper steeping time.

Whenever possible, ask for a taste sample before buying teas. While one can often tell much from the dried leaf and the smell of the brewed leaf, the ultimate test is in the mouth. Although there are many exceptions about colour, your tea merchant should be able to tell you what to expect. If the brew of a green tea is dark gold or orange-amber, it may be a low-quality tea. Most high-quality greens should brew up pale green to yellow-green. Brewed leaves should have a clean 'chestnut' flavour plus a pleasant vegetative flavour, and the better ones will have even more complexity.

Can't quite make the transition from tea bags to loose leaf? To make sure your box of tea bags is fresh, remove one bag and take out the tea. Pour hot water over just the paper tea bag. If the ensuing infusion tastes just like water, hooray. If it tastes more like tea, uh-oh—the paper has absorbed the flavour and the tea is simply too old.

How to store green tea

The enemies of tea are light, moisture and odours from other foods, so a tightly constructed opaque container is quite important, and its size should match the amount of tea. If too little tea is put into a large container, the tea will continue to oxidise. Glass and ceramic are totally inert and very good for teas; tins often leak because they have been soldered. Tea can be stored at room temperature, but if you live in a very humid or a very hot, dry environment, store your packages of tea in cool, dry, dark cupboards for extra protection.

Refrigerate or not?
Some green tea sellers recommend refrigeration, but so much depends upon packaging: storing tea in the refrigerator makes it very vulnerable to odours and moisture. If you have the advantage of a very stable storage unit, and it can be used only for tea, you might consider that. Temperatures should be kept between 1° and 4°C (30° and 40°F), and you can store the tea for up to six months.

In general, forget about freezing unless you are confident that your high-quality greens have been packaged very carefully. Otherwise, the water condensation when defrosted can greatly damage the tea. Besides, the best protection for preserving tea is to buy it fresh, in season, and in small quantities—50–100g (2–4oz) at most. Since 25g (1oz) of tea should generate about fifteen to thirty cups, that should keep you going for a little while!

THE BASICS OF BREWING GREEN TEA

The first consideration in brewing green tea is to think of it as a delicate food, to be handled tenderly, carefully and with respect. One can compare green tea to fresh leaf vegetables. Just as a chef handles produce gently, with grace, so should you handle tea. For example, if spinach is tossed into boiling water, the result is that much of the chlorophyll and the taste go into the cooking water, leaving you with shrivelled, overcooked leaves. However, if the leaves are gently laid in a steamer and water vapour is allowed to waft up, what results is a vegetable with more flavour and colour.

SELECTING THE WATER

Ideally, spring water that runs freely near where your tea grows is the best water to use. Since that's nearly impossible for those of us who live outside the green tea centres of Asia, bottled spring water is our best choice.

It is critical that the bottled water be spring water, taken directly from its source. Some find bottled waters are so pure and so free of minerals that they make a very flat tea. Many excellent bottled waters are available from Britain, Ireland, France, Italy and Switzerland, but their mineral content varies enormously. Just as you must use your palate to guide you to teas that taste best to you, you must taste waters and decide which ones bring out the best flavour in your teas without making them flat-tasting, chemical-tasting, or off-tasting in any way.

Never use distilled water; it has minerals taken out of it that are essential to bringing out the flavour of tea and will always make your tea flat. Distilled water is for your irons, not tea.

BUYING, STORING AND BREWING

The third choice would be to use a good filter system on your tap or a commercial filtering jug. Both are quite adequate.

MEASURING THE WATER AND TEA

Before brewing tea, always fill a measuring cup with water (300ml/ ½pt) and pour the water into your tea cup or pot to determine exactly how much water it holds. The styles and shapes of cups and pots vary tremendously. One pot may look small and actually hold 350ml (12fl oz) or a pot may look generous and yet actually only hold 165ml (6fl oz).

Now that you know how much water your vessel can hold, you can gauge the amount of tea to use. The ratio of tea to water is based on weight, because a teaspoon of smaller leaves literally weighs more than a teaspoon of larger leaves. Using equal amounts of water, a teaspoon of large leaves might give you an insipid drink, while a teaspoon of small, dense leaves would give you a satisfyingly strong cup of tea.

It is always a good idea to purchase a well-calibrated scale, or a well-built small food scale. A teaspoon is simply not as accurate a measuring tool as a scale. It is important to repeat that the larger the leaves the more you will use; the smaller, denser, leaves require smaller quantities. This is probably the most critical point to learn in brewing tea: Always measure your tea. If you drink the same type all the time, the amount will become second nature to you, but until then, learning how to use a fine scale that indicates both grams and ounces will make the measuring simple.

A second critical point is to always weigh the tea to match the amount of water you will be using. Vessels vary so much in the amount they can hold. Once you become accustomed to your teapot or cup, and how each of your favourite green teas should taste to you, this, too, will become much simpler.

Five grams of tea to 150ml (5fl oz) of water is best for brewing tea in a small teapot or large chong. Six grams of tea to 230ml (8fl oz) of water is best for every other method. The smaller guywans or covered bowls take three grams of tea for 120ml (4fl oz) of water. Good quality tea leaves sink to the bottom after they have infused, so one can drink directly from the guywan, or pour the liquor into smaller cups.

Tea drinkers quickly learn to be quite flexible. Tea is not an exact beverage; the exceptions are the rules. Trust your palate. Whenever you are not sure about amounts, use your tea merchant's guidelines. You can always adjust to your own tastes from then on.

Learning how to brew tea is not unlike the answer to the age-old question 'How do you get to Leicester Square?'

'Practise, practise, practise!'

STEEPING THE TEA

Lu Yu's dictum on boiling water for tea has become standard, especially in China, where the 'turbulent' waves of boiling water are for pu-erh, the pearls are for oolong and blacks, and the fish eyes are the right temperature for green tea. Pu-erh, an intentionally aged black tea from China, is the only tea that really requires roiling boiling water. Most blacks and oolongs do best with nearly boiling water, about 91–93°C (195–200°F), although the lower temperatures are best for oolongs and the higher temperatures are best for blacks.

For greens, much lower temperatures are absolutely essential to get the best flavour and the most infusions. Suggested temperature range is from 71–76°C (160–170°F), although some jasmines benefit from slightly higher temperatures (79–85°C; 175–185°F). Brewing green tea with cooler water and a shorter brewing time results in a better flavour in the brew. Covering the pot is also critical to helping the tea leaves unfurl, and will provide multiple infusions every time.

DETERMINING BREWING TIME

Generally, thirty seconds to one minute of steeping is best for greens, but there are some exceptions. Some Ceylon, Vietnamese, Nepalese and Indian greens—particularly Nilgiri and Darjeeling greens—can stand longer brewing times, and some Chinese Long Jing (Dragonwell) do quite well at six or seven minutes of brewing. Always ask your tea merchant for recommendations on time and temperature.

BUYING, STORING AND BREWING

Use a thermometer. Gauging the temperature of water quickly becomes a matter of being sensitive to your tea-kettle and the sounds it makes. Until you reach that feeling of familiarity, get yourself a simple sugar thermometer; they are available in most hardware stores, chef's shops or major supermarkets.

To determine water temperature, simply dip the metal gauge into the water, wait a few seconds for the temperature dial to move, and you can read the temperature. If it has reached its peak, remove the kettle from the heat source. If not, continue to heat until it is right. If you do this two or three times, you will be able to gauge the time and temperature easily, but you can always tell for sure with the thermometer.

You will soon become so familiar with your kettle that you will hear the bubbles as they grow from tiny to large to roiling. As with everything worthwhile, it just takes a little practice.

Breaking the 'crust'. Having said all the above, I must confess these are my personal opinions for the truest, sweetest, clearest infusions for green tea. Some tea merchants, far more experienced than I, continue to suggest that the water nearly reach the boiling point, if only to liberate or free up the oxygen content or 'break the oxidised crust'. The water is then allowed to cool to the suggested lower temperature, and then the steeping begins.

I suggest you try both methods: (1) heat to near boiling, then cool to 79–85°C (170–185°F) and infuse; or (2) heat only to 79–85°C (170–185°F) and infuse immediately. As Confucius said, 'Let your palate be your guide.'

CHAPTER 9

Serving

> Tea is naught but this:
> First you heat the water,
> Then you make the tea,
> Then you drink it properly.
> That is all you need to know.
> Sen-no Rikyu

If the first consideration for preparing tea is to buy well and use the best water at the right temperature, the second is to brew it in a vessel that is appropriate to the tea itself.

Brewing in small teapots

Very small one-cup porcelain teapots provide an excellent way to brew your tea. Green tea should always be infused without a strainer, tea ball, or any other constricting device so that the tea is able to unfurl easily and open up to its fullest flavour and aroma.

To use a one-cup teapot, pour in hot water and cover with the lid to warm the pot. Do the same with your cup; pour hot water into it, and cover with its saucer. Pour out the water from the teapot, place your weighed green leaves inside, and cover with the measured amount of hot water. Let steep for thirty seconds and taste. If it is satisfactory, continue through the next steps.

Empty your cup of water. Pour off all brewed liquor from the pot into your cup and drink. If there is more liquor in the pot than your cup can hold, pour off what remains into a jug or an empty teapot. Do not allow the liquor to remain on the leaves while you sip your first cup because oversteeping will cause the tea to become bitter.

SERVING

Most high-quality green tea will make three to eight infusions, and each subsequent infusion will be slightly different. Some teas get stronger and richer, others get more delicate, but each is a surprise and a delight. You can also experiment by increasing the time slightly for subsequent infusions, adding fifteen to thirty seconds each time to bring out different taste notes.

If using a small teapot for several people, serve each of your guests in the Chinese style, pouring a little in each cup down the line and back again, to ensure that everyone will have the same tea to taste. Brew the green tea leaves loose so that all the flavour can be released, and strain through a wire or bamboo infuser to recapture the leaves. Put the strained leaves back into the pot and pour more hot water on them to reinfuse. As always, make sure that all infused liquor is poured from the teapot every time you use it. Pour extra into a serving jug or extra teapot and pour seconds to guests from that prior to making another infused pot.

YIXING POTS

Yixing pots are the classic teapots that have been used since before 1500. Some were on the original tea ships sent to Europe, so they have been travelling around the world for centuries. The porous quality and longevity of these pots is astounding. It has been suggested that the red clay used for the British 'Brown Betty' may be similar to the clay of Yixing because both have superior heat retention capability, permeability and high plasticity. The differences are that most Brown Bettys are glazed whereas Yixing pots are not, and Brown Bettys are fairly new compared to the centuries-old Yixing teapots.

Yixing, on Lake Taihu, about 100 miles west of Shanghai in Jiangsu province in eastern China, does indeed have unusual clay and exceptional pottery methods honed over many centuries. The clay is beaten for up to three days to get as much of the air as possible out of it so that it will be strong and 'tight'. Pots can take firing from 1100 to 1350°C (2012 to 2462°F) and it is not unusual for the heating time to be more than forty hours for a single piece.

Yixing pots date from the Ming dynasty (1368–1644), and thousands have survived since then. They are highly collectable for both their whimsical designs and their sleek, elegant forms, which seem as contemporary as anything on the market today. Animals, flowers (especially the lotus) and unique shapes are all part of the fun of these pots, but the main reason for using them is that they bring out the best in fine tea.

The most highly prized colour is dark brown (*zisha* or purple sand) but the most common is the terracotta red. 'Zisha' is often used generically to describe any Yixing colour, but connoisseurs reserve the term to describe the smooth dark brown shade. The clay has naturally coloured ores that are sometimes arduously scraped out to fashion pots of ochre, black or teal. The teal ones are oxidised to heighten the colour, so keep these only for your collection; they are not suitable for drinking from. Teal decorative details are harmless, however. It should also be noted that some teapots get their colour not from the ore itself, but are painted ochre, black or teal. You can always tell the true colour simply by looking inside the pot.

Whenever purchasing a Yixing pot for brewing tea, ask how it pours. Some designs are adorable, but they simply don't function all that well for pouring the tea. The best pots to use are the ones with the traditional, classic designs. Prices vary from less than £20 for machine-made pots to thousands of pounds for those that are handmade by 'national treasure' ceramic artists. Antique pots are priceless in many cases, and some have been valued at more than £100,000. Look for chop marks on the bottom of the pot that identify the maker or designer. If they are in Chinese, ask the dealer to identify the source for you, or check a porcelain reference guide. You can certainly find a well-designed, beautiful handmade pot for around £50 that will last decades with proper care.

Because Yixing pots are made without an interior glaze, one should always use the same kind of tea in the same pot—e.g., always green tea in one pot, always oolong in another. If not, the previous brew will contaminate the present one, and you will not be able to enjoy the full benefits of flavour, aroma and visual perfection.

Some tea connoisseurs have pots for certain types of teas within each category, thus having a pot only for Long Jing (Dragonwell) and another just for Pi Lo Chun. The reason is that after years of brewing the same teas in the same pot, they can literally put in only water, and the flavour, aroma, and taste of years of tea will come through in the water without any tea leaves being used at all.

How to season your Yixing pot

Yixing teapots are largely made in the same way they have been for centuries. Sometimes a simple paraffin wax is applied to improve the look of an inexpensive pot, so if your pot has any wax on the surface, it should be removed. Place a terry cloth or linen cloth in the bottom of a heavy pan, put the teapot on one side and the lid on the other, and cover both completely with cold water. Bring the water to the boil and keep it boiling over a low heat for five to thirty minutes. This not only removes the wax, but sterilises the pot. Gently remove the pot from the water and allow to cool a little.

Next, you should season the pot with the type of tea you will always want to brew in it. Brew a strong pot of that tea and let the tea remain in the pot until it gets cool. Empty the pot, rinse with water and brew again. Let the pot cool and empty again, removing all the tea leaves. Alas, these two seasoning brews are not that great to drink, so feed your plants with both liquor and leaves.

Dry the pot carefully or allow to air-dry completely, with the lid off, after each use. If the lid is replaced too soon, it may encourage mould. Never use soap, never put it in the dishwasher, and only use cool or warm water to rinse your precious Yixing teapot.

Yixing as art

It is thrilling to enter a gallery and see ceramic art that is hundreds, sometimes thousands, of years old, yet seems contemporary. That remains one of the most remarkable experiences of viewing art, and the ceramic art of teapot design is no exception.

Many teapot lovers travel to Hong Kong every year to add to

their growing collections of Yixing teapots. The more adventurous take the trek to Yixing, to buy directly from the centuries-old factories that create these outstanding teapots.

Fortunately, you need not travel to China or Taiwan for your Yixing pleasures because more and more fine pots are now available in the West. In the United States, many galleries, recognising the pleasure and profit of these incredible ceramic vessels, have invited contemporary Yixing artists to show their works, drawing both rave reviews and dedicated collectors. While many tea suppliers offer Yixing teapots, those shown in galleries are often quite unique and have the extra reward of being signed by the artist.

Should you have the opportunity to visit Hong Kong, do go to the Flagstaff House Museum of Tea Ware in Hong Kong Park. In Taiwan, visit the Pinglin Tea Museum for extraordinary examples of both ancient and modern Yixing ware, which includes not only teapots, cups, tea bowls, tea boats and related tea service accessories but also bonsai pots, calligraphy accessories, and even roof tiles, all made from the famous clay of Yixing.

GUNG FU SETS

At Taiwanese tea shops and Chinese tea rooms, you will find *gung fu* tea sets, and often demonstrations of gung fu tea service, from the Chinese phrase that means 'the art of doing things well'. Anyone who has witnessed a well-trained tea server—with a lovely hand embracing the tiny pot, and a delicate index finger holding the lid in place—will tell you this is grace personified. In smooth, flowing movements, servers make this simple beverage of leaf and water seem like a spiritual experience that whisks you away from the daily cares and into the realm of 'teadom'.

In Taiwan, gung fu sets are used only for oolong teas as a way of offering small sips of this intensely flavoured, aromatic tea. But the beauty and art of such service has become popular as a way of serving all types of teas, including green tea. Purists may disagree, but gung fu is not only a simple, beautiful way to serve green tea; it is very practical too.

Because most gung fu pots are made of the porous Yixing

'purple clay', one must again assign only one type of tea to each pot, and never, ever mix them. The porous quality of such unglazed pots makes them absorb odours quite readily, and after many years one would be able to pour only hot water into a well-used pot and taste the tea. To use different teas would create unpleasant tastes that would ruin the integrity, not to mention the taste, of fine tea. Never clean a gung fu teapot with anything but water. No soap, no baking soda. Nothing.

A gung fu set can be quite simple or complex, but it usually contains a small teapot, two to four small 'thimble cups', a bowl to set them in, and a pitcher for extra tea or water. Some thimble cups come with matching saucers, and some sets have matching utensils for putting tea in the pot, and a tea caddy. The pot and cups are made of the classic Yixing unglazed clay, but the utensils can be made of bamboo, ceramic, or other materials. Other accessories might include a drainer to pour off unneeded water or tea and to store the spent leaves. These drainers can be porcelain, stainless steel or ceramic. The reason for all of these pieces is to make each step of serving tea elegant.

Gung fu service

Gung fu service for oolong tea begins with a rinsing of the leaves, in which hot water is poured onto the dried leaves to 'awaken' them (this is rarely necessary for green teas, although it is not uncommon to rinse Tianmu Mountain teas).

The liquor is immediately poured off, and hot water is poured over the wet leaves and left to steep from thirty seconds to several minutes, depending on the type of tea. Every time tea is brewed, its entire liquor is poured off. If allowed to remain on the leaves, the liquor will become bitter or overly astringent. If there is more liquor than there are cups to fill, the liquor is poured off into a small jug, similar to a creamer, and from that, refills are poured into each person's cup.

How the cups are filled is important. If several cups are being used, the host pours from left to right and right to left until they are all evenly filled. In this way, each guest receives the same quality of tea. If the cups were filled completely, one at a time, the last person would have a cooler cup than the first, and his tea would taste slightly different from the others. This is a gesture of hospitality, but more than that, respect for the tea.

TYPES OF DRINKING VESSELS

In the Chinese culture of tea, it is important to be able to smell and view the tea in its dried state, to see it infuse to its resulting liquor, and, always, to savour its taste. There is much beauty in a cup of green tea, due to the many shapes the leaves have—curled balls that unravel slowly like an awakening flower, or long, twisted shapes that unwrap to show off full leaves, or curved little leaves, called eyebrow teas, which, steeped, provide flavoursome tea like no other.

The colour spectrum of the tea liquor is astonishing, from palest celadon, almost clear, to a pale yellow-green, to an intense chartreuse or brilliant yellow, and many gradations in between. Despite its apparent delicacy, green tea is a palate cleanser. It goes wonderfully with spicy foods, yet drunk alone it is both energising and relaxing.

Tea cups

One of the ideal ways to serve green tea is in a white or pale celadon cup whose 'non' colour helps one to appreciate the slight variations of colour in the infused tea leaves and the various degrees of colour in the liquor.

Many Chinese people use porcelain covered cups called *guywan*. These are ideal because they do not keep the tea so hot that it is uncomfortable to drink, the saucer protects the hands, and the cover becomes a clever paddle to push the leaves gently back and forth to help them infuse fully. The nearly transparent porcelain is made of a pale green or white, a wonderful foil to enhance and reflect the colour and shape of the tea unfurling in the water, and the resulting pale liquor.

Guywan come in many patterns. They are readily available at

SERVING

Chinese shops and are quite modest in price, from a few pounds to less than £20. *Chongs*, or *chungs*, are larger than guywan, used as vessels more often than to drink out of, and are certainly more common for brewing oolongs than greens. Occasionally a shop owner might use the word *hu* to mean vessel or teapot, which can be applied to any vessel used to pour tea. *Zhongs*—handleless, mug-sized covered cups—are quite common in Chinese stores, but they take a great deal more water, usually about 300ml (½pt), and are more suitable for black teas. Taiwanese call covered cups *gaibei*.

Modern Chinese or Taiwanese cups are often terracotta or matt black on the outside, but have white porcelain interiors to show off the tea and the performance—the magical dance—as the leaves unfurl from their dried state to provide their precious liquor.

The Japanese often reserve the thinnest, palest of their porcelain cups for superior green tea; some cups are round, some have slight curves, others are elliptical, fitting into one's hand like a delicate creature. The near-translucent quality of these exquisite cups adds enormously to the pleasure of the complete experience of drinking green tea, accentuating the appreciation of all the factors—colour, aroma and taste. Here, again, the preferred colour is pale green or white. Many Japanese cups are handed down from generation to generation because of their exceptional artistry.

Tea glasses

One of the simplest yet most dramatic ways to drink green tea is in a glass tumbler. The effect of seeing the leaves infused is what makes this method so fascinating. Place about 3 grams of leaves in the glass and fill with about 120ml (4fl oz) of water heated to 65°C (150°F). Allow to brew about five minutes.

Using wine goblets is another way to brew green tea, especially for showing off mudans—rosettes of green leaves tied together with other leaves or silk threads. When infused, these rosettes 'blossom' into peony-shaped flowers. Mudans are sometimes referred to as peonies, sea anemones, or mutans, and the shapes and styles are endless. This is particularly riveting to entertain guests who can watch their tea 'bloom' during dinner, and then drink it with dessert. Fun!

Utensils

The Chinese use very simple, supremely functional accessories to make serving tea easy yet elegant. The following are some items you will find in shops selling Chinese goods. They will indeed make serving Chinese green teas more enjoyable.

Drainer. Available in porcelain or stainless steel, a drainer consists of a round tray, about 5cm (2in) or higher, and a lid that has holes in it, thus the eponymous name. Tea cups are placed on top of the drainer, and water is poured onto them to warm them. To eliminate the water, it is simply poured through the draining holes. Now the cups are warmed and ready for tea. The other function for the drainer is for pouring off excess tea. Also, when tea is concluded, the spent tea leaves can be emptied into the tray, to be disposed of neatly. Some drainers are about 23cm (9in) in diameter and others are about 30cm (12in) in diameter or larger.

Jug. These can be of various sizes, but small porcelain creamers are perfect. They are used for holding and then pouring extra hot water onto the tea leaves, or, if only serving to one or two people, they can be used to hold extra tea to avoid bitterness from too long an infusion.

Scale. For premier teas, a scale is an ideal way to determine the weight of tea that should be used. This is best done 'off site' if you have guests, unless the company is very informal or your scale is very striking.

Spout scraper. This is used to pull away any leaves stuck in the spout of a teapot.

Tea caddy. Porcelain, wood, Yixing clay or bamboo are typical materials for these boxes, which come in a myriad shapes and sizes, from the sedate to the whimsical. They are used to hold the teas during a tea service, and are not appropriate for storage. They make a nicer presentation than placing commercial boxes or bags of tea on your table.

SERVING

Terrycloth or linen towel. Towels are useful to discreetly sop up any water on the bottom of the serving teapot, or to blot up any drips of tea or water not caught by the drainer. Can also do double duty as a coaster for resting a hot teapot or kettle on a table.

Tools. These are usually bamboo, and come with their own vase, but porcelain ones are available. Included are:

Tea scoop or caddy spoon. Used for scooping and measuring tea. It is usually about 10cm (4in) long and about 2.5cm (1in) wide and has a lip at the end to contain the leaves. Antique ones were frequently shells for scooping out tea, and modern ones are bamboo. European versions are usually silver.

Tongs or pincer. This tool is used to lift cups that are too hot to handle when they are initially warmed with hot water.

CHAPTER 10

Wellness

Tea is a miraculous medicine for the maintenance of health. Tea has an extraordinary power to prolong life. Anywhere a person cultivates tea, long life will follow.

Eisai, *Kitcha Yojoki* (1211)

The Japanese philosopher Myo-ei Shonin of Toga-no-o once wrote on his kettle what he considered the virtues of tea:

The ten virtues of tea

1. Has the blessing of all the deities.
2. Promotes filial piety.
3. Drives away the devil.
4. Banishes drowsiness.
5. Keeps the five viscera* in harmony.
6. Wards off disease.
7. Strengthens friendships.
8. Disciplines body and mind.
9. Destroys passions.
10. Gives a peaceful death.

Since 230 BC doctors and monks have noted the many benefits of tea, particularly green tea. Its ability to offer refreshment, increase alertness and stave off disease consistently has been noted for thousands of years. Yet it is reassuring to know that pharmacologists, chemists, physicians, nutritionists, and others in the field

---

* The liver is said to like acid taste, the lungs pungent, the heart bitter, the spleen sweet, and the kidneys salt.

of health science are recognising the health-giving properties of tea when used consistently all through life.

Studies of tea's value in maintaining good health have been conducted and reported in medical journals throughout the world. Most notable have been studies conducted by the *Journal of the Japanese Society of Food Science and Technology*, Tufts University, Harvard University, the American National Cancer Institute and US teaching hospitals such as Johns Hopkins and Reed College. All of these studies concur on one point: green tea is an inexpensive, health-giving drink with possible long-range benefits, especially if taken daily throughout a lifetime.

The studies suggest that green tea may help lower the risk of cancer, inhibit ageing, reduce the risk of cardiovascular disease, help lower blood sugar levels, fight viral infections and even prevent tooth decay, bad breath and gum disease. While drinking green tea will certainly cause no harm, the best reason to drink it is because it does have time-tested benefits such as antioxidation of fats and possible anticancer properties.

Tea promotes general good health

Articles in the *University of California at Berkeley Wellness Letter* have indicated that green tea can be a protective, preventative drink. It is well known that it contains enough fluoride to help prevent tooth decay and is also rich in polyphenols, which act as antioxidants. Vitamins C and E and beta-carotene are also prevalent in tea. Provided it is not drunk scalding hot, green tea has been connected to a lower risk of oesophageal cancer, particularly in people who do not smoke or drink alcohol.

CHEMICAL COMPOUNDS FOUND IN TEA LEAVES

Many pharmacologists and medical practitioners now recommend three to four cups of green tea per day for such possible benefits as described. However, significantly more might be needed to achieve positive effects. **Do not self-prescribe, especially if you are a heart, diabetes or cancer patient.**

GREEN TEA

The percentages listed below are the amounts found in dry tea leaves. In addition to these compounds, there are about 500 different aromatic oils in the leaves of tea, which contribute to both aroma and taste and vary depending on the area in which the tea is grown. Pigments found in green tea are primarily green from chlorophyll; some red and yellow are derived from anthocyanins and flavones.

Compound	Concentration	Description
Antioxidants		A general classification of biochemical compounds that can prevent or fight cancer-causing cells. See polyphenols.
Caffeine	2–4 per cent	Revives the spirits, strengthens the heart, acts as a diuretic, increases metabolic rate, helps prevent asthma and boosts the central nervous system. Can increase alertness without the jitteryness of the caffeine in coffee and colas (which are assimilated into the body more quickly).
Carotene	13–29mg	Resists oxidation and mutation; reduces cholesterol levels; prevents high blood pressure, high blood sugar, infections and allergies to food; deters bad breath. See polyphenols.
Flavonols	0.6–0.7 per cent	Help increase immune system, strengthen capillaries, resist oxidation, lower blood pressure and help eliminate body odour.
Fluoride (fluorine)	90–350ppm	A mineral that helps prevent caries and strengthens tooth

		enamel. As little as one cup of green tea a day can help reduce plaque formation and bacterial infections in the mouth.
Glycosides	0.6 per cent	A broad range of chemical compounds found in plants, having a wide range of effects on the body, such as preventing an increase in blood sugar and acting as an antidiabetic.
Hetero chain polysaccharide	0.6 per cent	An element alleged to help prevent diabetes.
Magnesia	400–2,000ppm	Prevents oxidation and strengthens immune system.
Polyphenols	10–25 per cent	Chemical compounds that prevent oxidation and mutation of cells in the body. Anticarcinogenic, they help lower cholesterol levels and blood pressure, retard coagulation of red blood cells, help eliminate body odours, and help prevent food allergies.
Saponia	0.1 per cent	While only a trace amount is found in tea, it is known as an anticarcinogen and prevents inflammation associated with infections. Also known as saponin.
Selenium	1.0–1.8ppm	May help prevent oxidation, cancer and heart attacks.
Theanine	0.1 per cent or less	One of a very small group of amino acids found in tea.

Vitamin B-2 (riboflavin)	1 per cent or less	Appears in trace amounts.
Vitamin C	150–250mg	A powerful antioxidant that can help prevent scurvy and, possibly, degeneration of cells that can cause cancer. Does not exist in black tea because it is oxidised away.
Vitamin E	25–70mg	A compound that can help prevent oxidation of cells in the body and, possibly, degeneration of cells that can cause cancer. It is also a powerful vitamin that may delay the effects of ageing in both men and women.
Zinc	30–75ppm	Prevents abnormal indigestion, skin infections and suppressed immunity.

TEA REDUCES CANCER RISK

Of particular interest are the studies that indicate that green tea helps reduce the risk of cancer. Since 1987, pharmacologist Hasan Mukhtar, PhD, has presented nearly forty papers on the efficacy of green tea as an anticarcinogen. His experiments have been done primarily at Case Western Reserve University in Ohio. Inspired by the work done by Chinese scientists on green tea, he has made countless laboratory experiments that have demonstrated a link between green tea and the reduction of tumours and cancer-causing cells.

According to Dr Mukhtar, one probable reason for the anticancer quality of green tea is its chemo-preventative agent, polyphenols. These are well-documented powerful antioxidants that help control the activity of free radicals, the unstable compounds that can destroy cells and are implicated in a host of diseases, not just cancer, as well as premature ageing. By neutralisation, these free radicals are rendered harmless, but it is not yet known how and why antioxidants work.

Remarkably, Dr Mukhtar found that it did not matter where the green tea came from or whether the laboratory animals drank it hot or cool; the green tea always had a positive effect in reducing cancerous growths.

Current research using topical applications on humans shows great potential, and Dr Mukhtar hopes to explore more fully the effect of green tea on humans with existing cancers. And, yes, he drinks green tea himself these days, usually three or four cups a day.

The *American Journal of Epidemiology* reported that a study of 35,369 women and their incidence of cancer during an eight-year period linked regular tea-drinking with a lower risk of cancers of the upper digestive tract, colon and rectum. Drinking two or more cups of tea daily appeared to reduce the risk of cancer.

In a British study, positive results have also been attributed to using tea to combat tumours of the colon, liver, pancreas and mammary glands. It is interesting to note that the amounts of tea used were not megadoses but only about four cups per day.

Studies in Japan

A country noted for its excessive cigarette smoking, Japan ironically has a relatively low lung-cancer rate. To further confound logic, cigarette smokers in Japan have a 45 per cent lower risk factor than American smokers.

Although diet is a consideration, this striking difference between Japanese and American smokers has repeatedly been attributed to the generous consumption of green tea by the Japanese. Not unexpectedly, typical consumption levels of green tea in Japan are four to five cups a day, and sometimes more. The Japanese have for years highlighted the nutritional value of green tea, noting its high quantities of vitamins A and C and its alkaline properties, which are known to counteract the undesirable effects of acids contained in fish and meat.

The Japanese people also have significantly lower risks for cancers of the liver, pancreas, breast, oesophagus and skin, and researchers now believe the high consumption of green tea may play a large role in preventing these other forms of cancer.

In the Shizuoka prefecture, which cultivates tea as it has for nearly twelve centuries, the incidence of cancer is unusually low, even by Japanese standards. The residents of the area drink about ten small cups a day and use tea leaves only once, rather than brewing several infusions from the same leaves as most Japanese do. This is another intriguing piece in the puzzle of how and why green tea is beneficial. Since most of the evidence supporting green tea's benefits has been acquired by studying groups of people who, like those in the Shizuoka prefecture, consume great amounts of tea, we cannot definitely state that drinking just one to three cups per day will have the same positive effects.

TEA DELAYS THE AGEING PROCESS

In *The Green Tea Book*, Dr Lester A. Mitscher examines the results of many experiments that point out green tea's efficacy. Medical laboratory experiments with green tea suggest that putting an extract of green tea into the drinking water of animals helps their intrinsic antioxidant defence system become more effective. This is demonstrated by an increase in antioxidant enzymes, with particular improvement in the lungs, skin, lower intestine and liver.

Because cancer researchers have concluded that some cancers are the consequence of the accumulation of cell damage often caused by free radicals, it has been particularly important to discover the antioxidants that can fight these damaging free radicals. Green tea is loaded with the powerful antioxidants called polyphenols, particularly EGCG, epigallocatechin gallate, the most powerful.

EGCG has the ability to block the enzyme urokinase, which helps tumours grow by attacking neighbouring cells. EGCG effectively destroys urokinase's ability to destroy good cells.

Polyphenols' antioxidant ability helps cell DNA to reproduce itself accurately, rather than in a mutated form, and Chinese

Epigallocatechin gallate

medicines from tea polyphenols have long been used to treat nephritis, hepatitis and even leukaemia.

According to Professor Takuo Okada in the Pharmacology Department, University of Okayama, 'Green tea is more effective than Vitamin E. Vitamin E reduces the number of peroxide lipids, which slows down cell degeneration and the ageing process. Green tea has been shown to be twenty times more active in this respect than Vitamin E.'

TEA REDUCES THE RISK OF HEART DISEASE

In the United Kingdom, the Tea Council's own commissioned report resulted in similar findings on the benefits of tea drinking. Researchers discovered that four to five cups of tea a day might help reduce both high cholesterol and high blood pressure, and that both black and green teas were shown to inhibit ultraviolet B light-induced skin cancer in laboratory experiments with mice.

The British scientists also credit flavonoids and vitamins C and E with working against free radical damage to cells, and against oxidation of blood cholesterol, one of the main risk factors of heart disease.

Tea seems to work not only in reducing LDL-cholesterol oxidation but also in lowering overall blood cholesterol levels. Scientists suspect tea antioxidants enter the bloodstream, attach themselves to LDLs, and duplicate the body's own antioxidants that the LDLs eliminate in the aorta. These positive antioxidants then protect LDLs from oxidation and protect the artery walls from damage.

Eleven reasons to drink green tea

1. Lowers the risk of cancer.
2. Lowers the risk of cardiovascular disease.
3. Improves dental health and bone density.
4. Improves the fight against flu and other viral diseases.
5. Prevents infection.
6. Strengthens capillaries.
7. Reduces cholesterol, especially low density lipoprotein (LDL).
8. Natural diuretic.
9. Refreshing and relaxing.
10. Helps you focus and stimulates your thinking.
11. Tastes great.

Green tea supplements

If you don't want even the minimal caffeine of the recommended three to four cups of green tea a day, consider taking a supplement of green tea extract. Supplements generally contain about 500mg of green tea extract or the equivalent of five cups of green tea. They are rather expensive and you don't get the pleasure of drinking green tea, but you don't get the caffeine either. Try to select supplements made with a base of pure vegetable glycerine or refrigerated pure tea extract for freshness and potency. Otherwise you're just buying 'green stuff'.

CHAPTER 11

Beauty and Health

You can taste and feel, but not describe, the exquisite state of repose produced by tea, that precious drink, which drives away the five causes of sorrow.

Emperor Ch'ien Lung (1710–99)

One of the marvels of green tea is that not only is it a refreshing and delicious beverage, but it's good for you—inside and out. Beauty and health applications are quite varied, and in this chapter I shall suggest ways to include green tea in your daily hygiene regime. The natural astringency of green tea makes it both soothing and healing, and the steeped leaves have just enough gentle exfoliation properties to make your skin glow.

Green tea soother

This is a wonderful all-purpose astringent and an antibacterial solution. It is important to use unflavoured, unscented teas because perfumes, oils or flavouring agents might be harsh on minor injuries. This recipe is for a concentrated strength, not drinkable!

1 cup green tea (suggested green teas are sencha, gunpowder or Long Jing, but any will do)
1 litre (2pts) spring water

1. Brew tea in spring water either by heating water to 85°C (185°F) and steeping for 20 minutes or pouring room temperature spring water on the tea and steeping for about an hour.
2. Cool the liquid.
3. Pour into sterilised bottles and refrigerate. It is always best to

GREEN TEA

prepare small quantities and use promptly to ensure strongest potency.

USES FOR GREEN TEA SOOTHER:

- Use as a cooling, refreshing après bath splash; can be used either at room temperature or chilled.
- Perk up tired feet by splashing Green Tea Soother on them.
- For an antifungal foot bath, pour a litre (2pts) of Green Tea Soother into a bucket or shallow basin. Soak your feet for about fifteen minutes. Blot off excess but do not rinse. Cover your feet with fresh white cotton socks (to 'lock in' the antiseptic quality of the tea). This is excellent for toe fungus, athlete's foot or minor irritations of the feet from running, jogging, or standing for long periods of time. It's an ideal way to treat your feet prior to bedtime, but it can be done any time during the day.
- Use as a mouthwash.
- For minor cuts, rashes or abrasions, saturate a pure cotton pad with Green Tea Soother and apply directly to injury for at least five minutes. Repeat. This can be done up to four times a day. Repeat the next day, if necessary, but you should see healing at the end of the first day.
- To soothe minor sunburn, soak a piece of flannel or cotton cloth in the green tea solution and lay the cloth on the sunburned area. Keep the cloth on until the burned area begins to cool, about fifteen minutes.
- To freshen up strained or tired eyes, soak cotton pads in green tea solution, squeeze out excess, and lay them gently on your eyelids. Let the pads rest on your lids for about ten minutes. Repeat if necessary. This helps to reduce puffiness, red eyes, and eyes fatigued from reading, computer work or other close work.
- Use as a blemish remedy. Rinsing the face with tea has an astringent, healing effect on the skin. Green Tea Soother is great for pimples, but any concentrated extract

of green tea will work. Splash on the face, or dot onto blemishes with pure cotton. Do not rinse; allow the tea to do its work undiluted.

Green tea soap (*2 100g (4oz) bars*)

Soap-makers swear by tea. Leaves offer gentle abrasion to slough off dead skin, yet they are gentle for all skin types. The following is really a recycling recipe made from a collection of those itsy-bitsy leftovers of your favourite unscented soaps. If you cannot find matcha, crushed leaves or the fannings used in tea bags will give the soap just enough colour. If you're an experienced soap-maker, think tea for your next batch!

> 225g (8oz) white soap shreds
> 12g (½oz) green tea dust or matcha for colour (optional)
> 100g (4oz) steeped tea leaves (any kind)

1. Soak the soap bits in a bowl of water until softened. With a slotted spoon scoop them out into another bowl, add tea dust, and mix thoroughly until the soap becomes pale green with a thick consistency.
2. Fold in the tea leaves gently, mixing only enough to incorporate them into the mixture.
3. Strain in a sieve for about 20 minutes to eliminate as much water as possible, then pack into mini loaf tins or mini gelatine moulds and let dry for about 8 hours or overnight. Mini loaf tin soaps can be cut into smaller slabs; the mini moulds can be used as is, if small.

Green tea bath bags (*1–2 baths*)

The green tea leaves are a mild sloughing agent, and the comfrey or calendula will add a soothing touch. The result? Silky skin.

> 50g (2oz) loose leaf green tea
> 50g (2oz) calendula or comfrey (available from health food shops)
> 4–6 drops rose essential oil (optional)

GREEN TEA

1. Mix all ingredients thoroughly and fill sachets made from loosely woven 100 per cent cotton gauze (available from craft shops). Tie the tops with string or ribbon.
2. To use, hold under the running tap of a bath tub until bath is half full, and squeeze several times to release the fragrance.
3. Rub the tea bag gently over your body, paying special attention to elbows and knees and any other rough spots.
4. Allow the bag to float in the bath to add its skin-softening properties to the water.

Bath salts (*4 baths*)

340g (12oz) epsom salts
¼ teaspoon glycerine
15 drops pine or eucalyptus essential oil (or your own favourite)
⅛ teaspoon matcha green tea

1. Mix all ingredients well and air-dry for several hours. Store in an airtight container.
2. To use, measure out 125ml and pour into the bath while the water is running.

Anti-fungal foot powder (*¼ cup*)

This powder is excellent in your shoes, bedroom slippers, socks, or anywhere your feet are! Helps to keep feet healthy and fresh smelling.

12g (½oz) matcha green tea
1 tablespoon baking soda
12g (½oz) cornflour
9 drops patchouli or lavender essential oil

Mix all the ingredients together thoroughly. Store in glass spice jars, retaining the lids to make sprinkling easy.

BEAUTY AND HEALTH

Green tea mask (*1 mask*)

230ml (8fl oz) mayonnaise (freshly made or commercial)
1 heaped teaspoon matcha

1   Stir all ingredients together thoroughly.
2   Apply evenly all over the face, avoiding the eye area.
3   Rest, lying down for about twenty minutes.
4   Carefully wipe off mask. Rinse face thoroughly with tepid water about 20 times.
5   Pat dry lightly with a soft towel.
6   If you use the mask during the daytime, apply a light moisturiser after rinsing and drying. If you use the mask prior to bedtime, do not apply moisturiser as the natural oils that are released during the night will be enough to keep your skin soft and moist.

Green tea teeth cleanser

Green Tea Teeth Cleanser can be refrigerated in a covered container for up to three days, but it is best to use it fresh for the most beneficial effect.

25g (1oz) unscented green tea leaves (any kind)
230ml (8fl oz) spring water
1 teaspoon baking soda

1   Make an extract of green tea by pouring hot (about 185°F; 85°C) spring water on the green tea leaves. Allow to infuse for 20–30 minutes or longer.
2   Make a paste by mixing ½ teaspoon of the green tea extract with the baking soda.
3   Brush teeth as usual. Rinse thoroughly.

Repairing fingernails with tea bags

Now that you've discovered the pleasures of loose leaf green tea, do not despair of those tea bags in the cupboard. The gauzelike paper is fabulous for repairing and building up split artificial nails.

1–2 teabags
Clear nail polish
Coloured nail polish (optional)

1 Cut the tea bag paper to the shape of your nails.
2 Apply teabag to nail with clear polish and let dry.
3 Apply a coloured polish after the clear dries, if desired.

Aubrey's green tea moisturiser

This completely natural moisturiser is wonderful for very dry skin or for ageing and wrinkled skin. The oils are superb emollients, the green tea and lavender oils provide the astringent elements to keep skin firm and smooth, and the aloe vera is a soothing agent and natural hydrator. Apply lightly to the face morning and night, rubbing well into ageing areas of the skin.

This recipe is courtesy of Aubrey Hampton, who has a terrific line of organic beauty products.

1 teaspoon white camellia oil
1 teaspoon rosehip seed oil
1 teaspoon jojoba oil
1 teaspoon evening primrose oil
1 teaspoon St John's wort flower buds
¼ teaspoon citrus seed extract (grapefruit is suggested)
1 teaspoon milk thistle seed extract
3 tablespoons shea butter
2 teabags sencha
350g (12oz) tofu
4 tablespoons aloe vera gel
1 teaspoon flaxseed oil
16 drops lavender oil

1 Place the white camellia oil, rosehip seed oil, jojoba oil, evening primrose oil, St John's wort flowers, citrus seed extract, milk thistle seed extract and shea butter in a small,

BEAUTY AND HEALTH

clean saucepan. Add the teabags and heat gently over low heat.
2. As the shea butter melts and combines with the oils, press the teabags with a spoon to get as much of the tea as possible into the hot oils. When the mixture is just about to boil or the shea butter is completely melted, turn off the heat and allow the mixture to cool, again pressing tea out of the teabags. The colour should be a clear yellow-green.
3. Place the tofu in a blender and add the tea mixture. Blend until creamy and smooth. Add the aloe vera gel, flaxseed and lavender oils, and mix until completely integrated. The final cream should be a light oatmeal colour.
4. Pour the moisturiser into clean glass bottles or jars and refrigerate or keep cool until ready to use.

Tea for toothache

For temporary relief from toothache, place wet green tea leaves directly on the sore tooth. Pack it in and allow to rest in the mouth for twenty minutes. Remove the leaves, but do not rinse your mouth. This should ease the pain until you get to your dentist.

USING GREEN TEA AROUND THE HOUSE

Tea is a completely and wholly recyclable plant. No need to pour leftover tea down the sink or toss used leaves into the rubbish bin—recycle them. Green tea is especially wonderful as a deodorant that absorbs offensive odours, it's full of nitrogen that can feed the plants in your garden (ferns go wild for tea), and it even wards off pests and insects.

TEA AS A DEODORISER

Straw mats. In the hot, humid areas of Thailand, Burma and other Asian countries, people sleep on straw mats, sometimes referred to by the Japanese word *tatami*. The straw is cool and comfortable, but people do perspire. It is quite common in these areas for tatami to be washed in tubs of water to which tea has been added. The tea works as a powerful deodoriser, leaves a fresh scent, and can even infuse the straw with a delicate sage colour (or golden colour if black tea is used). You can also use tea to clean other washable surfaces, such as yoga mats and air mattresses.

Litter trays. Used green leaves are wonderful in cat litter as an extra boost for diffusing odours, and they help deter fleas from both cats and dogs.

Pet beds. Sprinkle dried used green tea leaves on your pet's favourite pillow or bed. Great in kennels or anywhere troublesome pet odours occur. If you can afford the extravagance, loose leaf gunpowder tea is great for dogs to roll around in. The crunching of the pellets releases a wonderful aroma, and helps to scratch wherever dogs have an itch. The pellets help give your dog a more pleasant smell.

Refrigerators. Place used green tea bags or leaves in a small bowl, uncovered, in your refrigerator to help absorb odours from onions and garlic for about three days. No need to throw them out even then, just sprinkle the old leaves around your ferns, rosebushes, or other plants.

Kitchen odours. Preparing fish? Cutting up garlic? Rid your hands of the fish or garlic oils by rubbing them with wet green tea leaves, an instant deodoriser. The leaves are also great for deodorising and cleaning the pan in which you cook fish or garlic.

QUENCH YOUR PLANTS

Pour leftover green tea directly into the pot of your favourite house-plants or garden plants. The nitrogen and other good elements of leftover tea liquor are perfect for your plants. You can layer the top of the pots with the wet, used leaves, and let them rot naturally into the dirt, regenerating it better than any commercial plant food you can buy.

INSECT REPELLENT

Mosquitos. Dried green tea leaves are especially good at repelling mosquitos. Put some in a fireproof container, light with a match, and set outside where mosquitos or flies congregate. If neces-

BEAUTY AND HEALTH

sary, add a piece of charcoal briquette to the leaves. The smoke from the burning leaves will smell pleasant to you, but not to the bugs.

Moths. Sachets of green teas are excellent to deter moths. Place sachets in your chest of drawers, or tie them with a ribbon and wrap around hangers to protect precious woollen clothing.

ICE IT!

Pour leftover green tea into ice cube trays to make green tea ice cubes. Add them to fruit juices for an extra tang, or make your next pot of green tea iced, and add the cubes for additional flavour without diluting the tea.

CLEAN RUGS

Whether you have wall-to-wall carpets or scatter rugs, you can revive their colours and clean them easily with tea. Spread dry green tea leaves all over the rug, rub in gently, and brush off thoroughly. Vacuum as usual. The carpets will not only be cleaner, but they'll smell fresher, too. This works well with either dried or redried leaves.

Green tea dye

Black teas have long been used in television and theatre to soften white clothing or create an antique appearance for fabrics. Green tea also works to add a pastel sage colour to any white or écru fabric.

    Green tea (any type)
    Water

1   Make an extract of green tea using 3 parts tea to 1 part water; brew at room temperature for about an hour.
2   Soak cloth or fabric item for 20 minutes; check for colour.
3   If colour is satisfactory, roll out liquid gently and air-dry. For more intense colour, allow to soak an additional 20 minutes.

CHAPTER 12

Green Tea in Cooking

Its liquor is like the sweetest dew from heaven.
Lu Yu, 'Ch'a Ching', *The Classic of Tea, Origins and Rituals* (AD 780)

PREPARING GREEN TEA FOR COOKING

Green tea is a wonderful ingredient in cooking. It adds a bite, a sparkle, to marinades, dressings and sauces. Green teas are great to cook with, and they are lovely to use as garnishes, dried or infused. A sprinkle of gyokuro atop a salad or a dash of crushed gunpowder in a vinaigrette is a unique way to perk up your meals and add that extra something that will cause your family or guests to sit up and take notice.

The trick of using green tea in cooking is to brew it in a different way from when it is prepared for drinking. Use cool spring water and loose leaf teas, and brew for twenty to thirty minutes in a cup right on your kitchen worktop. This time method prevents the tea from ever being overly astringent or bitter. A typical measurement is one and one-half heaped teaspoons (7.5ml) of green tea to 250ml (8fl oz) of water. Adjust to your taste.

MATCHING GREEN TEAS WITH FOODS

Just as a sommelier would suggest a particular wine for each dish on your menu, you might want to consider doing the same for matching green tea with your meals.

Green teas are, on the whole, cooling, refreshing and palate cleansing, so they're wonderful with any spicy cuisine. Chinese greens tend to be sweeter than Japanese, which are nonetheless subtle and mild. Indian and Sri Lankan greens are stronger and more solid-tasting, and hold up well with the spiciest foods. All are, of course, wonderful by themselves, but only the subtlest ones would be lost with dramatically spiced foods. This is truly a mix-and-match category.

Long Jing is readily available, and an ideal green tea to serve with any seafood salad. In fact, it makes a great garnish sprinkled on top of a salad. It is refreshing with most Chinese foods, whether Hunan, Szechuan or Cantonese.

Japanese green teas are good with typical foods of that country, and their mildness makes them refreshing with fruits, salads, or any cuisine. The very fine gyokuro is magnificent by itself, or lovely with fresh fruit or pastries. Spiderleg and sencha are good with main courses from sukiyaki to beef stew. Hojicha, bancha, and genmaicha are excellent for all ages to drink, and taste good with all foods because of their mild flavour and soft aroma.

Indian greens like Makaibari green, Reeshihat, Oothu, or the Taiwanese Jade Oolong are wonderful with Indian foods and others that can stand up to a bite of a brew.

Those greens with a hint of floral, like the orchid notes of a Taiping Huang or the whisper of peach in a Pi Lo Chun, are wonderful with desserts. And greens intentionally scented with jasmine, osmanthus, lychee or chrysanthemum are lovely as aperitif teas or with pastries. As always, let your palate guide you. The best way to determine what greens you like to drink with your foods is to try as many selections as possible. This is a wide open field for experimentation, so have fun with it. Rules simply don't exist, but the excitement of mixing flavours certainly does. If it tastes good to you, it will taste divine to your family and guests.

Salmon, watercress, and sencha 'soup' (*4 servings*)

This recipe calls for nori seaweed and wasabi—a strong, pungent Japanese green horseradish made by mixing water (or, in this case, green tea) with a powdered base. Both are available in the Japanese food section of most major supermarkets or in Asian natural food markets.

GREEN TEA

2½ rounded teaspoons sencha leaves (hojicha, or roasted bancha, can be used)
455ml (16fl oz) spring water
2 large salmon fillets, about 2cm (¾in) thick
1 tablespoon olive oil
white pepper to taste
450g (1lb) steamed rice, cooled
1 bunch watercress, chopped
½ teaspoon prepared wasabi
1 sheet toasted nori seaweed, cut into thin strips

1. Brew sencha in hot (76°C; 170°F) spring water for about two minutes. Decant immediately after it has been brewed; set aside.
2. Lightly brush the fillets with olive oil and sprinkle a pinch of white pepper on each side.
3. Grill salmon about 4 minutes on each side, depending on size. The fillets should flake easily with a fork when they are done.
4. Gently remove skin and bones, and shred the fillets with a fork.
5. Place rice in four deep bowls, arranging fish on top. Sprinkle with watercress. Pour hot brewed sencha into bowls until rice is nearly submerged.
6. In a small bowl dilute the wasabi with some of the same rice. Garnish the bowls of fish and rice with the nori and a tiny bit of the wasabi.
7. Serve immediately.

Chinese green tea chicken salad (*4 servings*)

This is a twist on the classic Chinese chicken salad, with green tea as a flavouring for the dressing. For extra flavour, the chicken can be cooked with the skin; remove the skin before adding chicken to the salad.

3 tablespoons sesame oil, divided
4 boneless chicken breasts

3 teaspoons fresh Chinese green tea leaves (Pi Lo Chun, Long Jing, or similar)
75ml (½ cup) cold spring water or rice vinegar
¼ teaspoon soy sauce
¼ teaspoon sugar
112ml (¾ cup) olive oil
½ cup slivered toasted almonds
1 can sliced water chestnuts, drained
1 head iceberg lettuce, torn into strips

1. Heat 2 tablespoons sesame oil in a large frying-pan over medium heat. Sauté the chicken breasts until cooked, about 5 minutes on each side. Set aside to cool.
2. To make the dressing, steep the tea leaves for about 20 minutes. (If using low-grade green teas, steep in rice vinegar; use cold water for a high-quality tea.) Strain and discard leaves. Add remaining tablespoon sesame oil, soy sauce, sugar, and olive oil; mix well.
3. Tear chicken into small pieces. Combine with slivered almonds, water chestnuts and lettuce. Add the dressing and serve immediately.

Green marbled eggs (*6–12 servings*)

This is a twist on the classic Chinese tea eggs recipe, using green tea instead of black. When the cracked shells are peeled, the egg whites will be a pale green in a pattern made from the cracked shell.

6 to 12 eggs
50ml (¼ cup) green tea (Jade Oolong or pouchong)

1. Boil eggs in a pot of water until hard-cooked, about 20 minutes. Remove from water and gently tap them to crack the eggshells all over.
2. Add the green tea to the water and heat the eggs gently for another 10 to 15 minutes. Remove and let cool.
3. Serve whole, or halve them and serve cut side down on some butter lettuce with a delicate mayonnaise-based dressing.

GREEN TEA

Omelette Gyokuro (*1 large or 2 small servings*)

3 large eggs
1 tablespoon water
1 pat butter
½ level teaspoon gyokuro leaves

1. In a medium-sized bowl, whisk together the eggs and water.
2. Place butter in a frying-pan or omelette pan and melt slowly over low heat. Gently pour the eggs into the pan.
3. When the eggs begin to settle, sprinkle the tea leaves evenly over the eggs. Gently fold in half and serve immediately with toast or plain rice.

Jade Oolong shrimp (*3 servings*)

2 tablespoons Jade Oolong or pouchong tea
230ml (8fl oz) spring water
1 dozen large shrimp
1 bunch greens of choice, washed and dried
1 teaspoon lemon zest for garnish
1 tablespoon chopped chives for garnish

1. Infuse tea in spring water for about 20 minutes.
2. Pour into skillet and heat gently over low heat. Poach shrimp in heated tea for 3 to 5 minutes, until shrimp turn pink; drain.
3. Wash and dry greens and arrange on a platter. Scatter shrimp over greens and garnish with lemon zest and chopped chives. A light vinaigrette can be sprinkled over the salad for extra punch. Serve with white rice.

Jasmine sorbet (*3 cups*)

Aromatic teas like jasmine are ideal for 'intermissions' of fresh sorbets between courses or for dessert. This is a cinch to make with an at-home ice-cream freezer, but you can make it without

GREEN TEA IN COOKING

one. The texture and consistency will be more like a sorbet and must be eaten the same day.

700ml (24fl oz) spring water
2⅓ tablespoons jasmine tea leaves
200g (7oz) sugar

1. Bring the water to the boil in a small saucepan. Remove from heat and slowly add the tea leaves. Cover and allow the tea to steep 5 minutes.
2. Add the sugar, stirring until dissolved. Taste; if necessary, add 2–3 more tablespoons sugar and stir until dissolved.
3. Strain the liquid over a bowl; discard tea leaves. Cover and chill about 2 hours.
4. Pour mixture into ice-cream maker, following manufacturer's directions. Or freeze in a bowl, covered with plastic wrap. Every hour for about 4 hours, uncover and stir the mixture with a fork.
5. Serve alone as an intermission; add some vanilla wafers if served as a dessert.

Cold tea noodles (*4 servings*)

This refreshing dish provides an easy escape from the kitchen on a sweltering day. Keep cool by cooking the noodles the night before. The next day, assemble the short list of ingredients and serve. Recipe courtesy of Chef Robert Wemischner of Los Angeles.

2.25l (4pts) water
1 teaspoon Japanese genmaicha
450g (1lb) Chinese water noodles or Japanese udon noodles
1 package (350g/12oz) firm tofu, well drained
1 small package enoki mushrooms
1 package radish sprouts, washed and dried
1 bunch spring onions, sliced into very thin rounds
1 small bunch coriander leaves
light soy sauce, to taste

Japanese sesame oil, to taste
shichimi togarashi (Japanese spice mixture, available in Asian food shops) or freshly ground black pepper, to taste

1. Bring water to 83°C (180°F) and add tea. Steep for 3 minutes and pour through a sieve. Reserve liquid for cooking the noodles.
2. Bring the reserved tea to the boil and add noodles. Cook for about 5 minutes, or until noodles are still somewhat al dente. Remove from heat and allow the noodles to remain in the liquid until cooled. Drain; place noodles in a covered bowl. Refrigerate overnight.
3. Before serving, place the tofu on a plate and cover it with several layers of paper towels. Press any excess moisture from it by placing an approximately 900g (2lb) weight on top of the towels. Remove weight and towels after 15 minutes. Discard any liquid that has accumulated. Carefully slice the tofu into 25mm (1in) cubes and set aside.
4. Place equal amounts of noodles on each of four plates. Scatter tofu, coriander, and vegetables evenly over all. Serve with soy sauce, sesame oil and seasoning.

Green tea-poached Chinese pears with pistachio cream sauce edged with a rumour of mint (*4 servings*)

This is a refreshing dessert with a touch of luxury that works all year round. Its complex taste belies its simple method of preparation. Recipe courtesy of Chief Robert Wemischner of Los Angeles.

4 Chinese pears, about 280g (10oz) each
5 teaspoons green tea leaves (Long Jing is ideal)
1 litre (2pts) spring water
100g (4oz) granulated sugar
1 5cm (2in) piece of fresh gingerroot, peeled and sliced into thin coins
peel of half a lemon
1 large sprig fresh mint

GREEN TEA IN COOKING

Pistachio Cream Sauce (recipe follows)
chopped pistachios and fresh mint leaves for garnish, if desired

1. Peel and core the pears, being sure to remove the tart centre core area of each. Brew tea by simmering in water for 5 minutes. Sieve out leaves and place resulting tea with sugar, gingerroot, lemon peel and mint in a saucepan large enough to hold the four pears in a single layer. Poach pears for about 20 minutes, or until somewhat tender (note that Chinese pears remain quite crisp even after cooking).
2. Remove the pears, sieve out solids, and return the sieved liquid to the saucepan. Reduce to a syrup by cooking over high heat for about 15 minutes. Put the pears back into the liquid and allow to cool. Refrigerate covered. Place four goblets or glass bowls in the refrigerator to chill.
3. Just before serving, remove pears from poaching liquid, drain well, and place one in each chilled goblet. Mask with the Pistachio Cream Sauce and serve immediately, garnished with chopped pistachios and fresh mint leaves, if desired. Plain thickened yogurt can be used instead of the sauce. To thicken, drain yogurt in a sieve until liquid stops dripping and the yogurt thickens.

Pistachio cream sauce (about 600ml (1pt))

100g (4oz) low fat plain yogurt, well drained
120ml (4fl oz) buttermilk
1 teaspoon golden syrup
100g (4oz) shelled and skinned pistachios (natural, no colouring), coarsely chopped

In a small bowl, whisk together the yogurt, buttermilk and golden syrup. Add the nuts and store mixture in refrigerator until serving time.

GREEN TEA

Green tea ice-cream (*about 10 one-scoop servings*)

This rich, classic Japanese dessert is a perfect marriage of thick cream with the mild astringent taste of a Japanese green tea, preferably a spiderleg or gyokuro. Spending a little extra for the best tea really makes a difference in the final product. A wooden spoon is important to avoid infusing the ice-cream with the taste of a metal spoon.

1 heaped teaspoon green tea leaves
230ml (8fl oz) cold spring water
5 large egg yolks
150g (6oz) sugar
230ml (8fl oz) full cream milk
500g (16oz) double cream
1½ teaspoons vanilla
½ teaspoon freshly grated lemon zest
pinch of freshly ground nutmeg

1. Brew tea leaves in cold spring water for about 30 minutes to best extract the green tea flavour. Remove leaves; cover and refrigerate.
2. Whisk the egg yolks in a medium-sized saucepan until creamy yellow, then add the sugar a little at a time, whisking slowly. Set aside.
3. In a small saucepan, combine the milk with half the double cream, stirring gently with a wooden spoon. Cook over low heat just until tiny bubbles form around the edge of the inside of the pan. Reduce the temperature and cook about 10 minutes, continuing to stir.
4. Next, combine the egg mixture with the cream. To avoid curdling the eggs, pour the hot cream mixture into the egg yolks very slowly, cooking over low heat. Stir constantly, until the mixture coats the spoon. Remove from heat. Stir in the vanilla. Allow to cool slightly, then pour into a large glass bowl, cover with plastic wrap, and refrigerate for about 4 hours.
5. Remove the chilled mixture from the refrigerator. Stir in the chilled tea liquor, lemon zest and nutmeg. Beat the remaining

double cream into stiff peaks and gently fold in to chilled mixture. Pour into an electric ice-cream maker and freeze, following manufacturer's directions.

Traditional matcha (*2 servings*)

Take several quick sips when drinking matcha. If drunk too slowly, the powder and water will begin to separate.

   1 teaspoon matcha
   150ml (5fl oz) spring water, heated to under boiling (88°C; 190°F)

1. Heat two tea bowls or small dessert bowls with hot water. Discard the water when bowls are warm to the touch. Wipe dry completely.
2. In a separate bowl, combine the matcha and heated water, and whip up the tea into a froth with a whisk. (A bamboo whisk is traditional, but a cooking whisk will do.) Pour into the warmed bowls and drink immediately. Chocolate or a sweet sugar biscuit is a nice accompaniment.

Matcha iced 'cappuccino' (*1 serving*)

   ½ teaspoon matcha
   1 teaspoon sugar (optional)
   100ml (3fl oz) heated spring water (about 88°C; 190°F)
   ice cubes

1. Whisk the matcha, sugar, and heated water until frothy.
2. Pour into a glass full of ice, and drink.

STASH COOLERS

The American Stash Tea Company has a fascinating selection of recipes for cooking with their tea bag teas on its web site, and they have generously shared them to inspire you to 'cool down with green tea'. The following drinks are easy to make with tea bags of premium green tea, but they can be adapted to include

GREEN TEA

concentrates of any fine loose-leaf green tea such as gunpowder, spiderleg, sencha, or your own personal favourite.

Stash tea premium green tea concentrate

1 bag Stash Premium Green Tea
50ml (2fl oz) boiling water

1. Place one bag of Stash Premium Green Tea in an 250ml (8oz) cup and pour boiling water onto the bag. Steep 4 to 6 minutes. Remove tea bag, squeezing out excess liquid.
2. Fill the cup with cold spring water. Double the recipe as necessary.

(To make a concentrate with loose-leaf green tea, follow the same directions but use one teaspoon of leaves in place of a tea bag. After brewing, remove the tea leaves and discard, or put them on your plants.)

Papaya nectar green tea (*4 servings*)

300ml (½pt) Stash Tea Premium Green Tea Concentrate (see recipe above)
300ml (½pt) papaya nectar (canned is OK)
3 teaspoons honey
ice cubes

Pour all ingredients into a blender with ice cubes and pulse until thick.

Moroccan mint tea (*6 small servings*)

This is a sweet drink that's perfect with the exotic cuisine of Morocco: hearty lamb stews, couscous, and generous condiments of nuts, apricots and dates. The tea is always served in small glasses, sometimes made of crystal, and often with brass holders. Upon entering a home, or even a place of business, one is automati-

GREEN TEA IN COOKING

cally given a glass of tea. Offering the tea is, simply and generously, a gesture of hospitality and welcome.

Of course, to be truly authentic one should have the *sinya*, a traditional three-legged tray, usually made of brass, plus a smaller tray on which three boxes are placed, one to keep the tea, one for the mint, and one for the sugar. A brass kettle is traditionally used to boil the water, which is used to heat the teapot; then the water is removed. What is produced is a highly concentrated green tea extract heavily sweetened, with a touch of spearmint. To western tastes, this may at first appear to be too sweet or too concentrated, but it is very calming and a wonderful digestive after meals.

If spearmint is hard to find, peppermint is acceptable. Spearmint is sweeter, softer, and more delicate tasting with the green tea. A better alternative is the mint found in most produce sections of your local grocery. It, too, is sharper than spearmint, but less so than peppermint.

3 teaspoons green tea (gunpowder is traditionally used)
700ml (1¼pt) water
15–20 sugar cubes
2 spearmint sprigs

1. Place the green tea in a teapot. Pour enough boiling water to cover the tea and 'awaken the leaves', then pour the water off.
2. Next, place the sugar cubes on the tea leaves and fill the pot to the halfway point with boiling water. Place spearmint sprigs on top just to offer an essence, and remove after about a minute.
3. The liquor is then poured into the small glasses and served. If you have no small glasses, serving the tea in cups is quite all right.

Glossary

Set a teapot over a slow fire;
Fill it with cold water;
Boil it long enough to turn a lobster red;
Pour it on the quantity of tea in a porcelain vessel;
Allow it to remain on the leaves until the vapour evaporates,
Then sip it slowly,
And all your sorrows will follow the vapour.
—Emperor Kien Lung

NOTE: Most pinyin Chinese terms reflect the pronunciation of the Mandarin dialect, which is spoken in Taiwan and in much of mainland China.

Bud. The top unopened leaf of a *Camellia sinensis* bush, prized for its tenderness and sweetness. It is generally considerably paler than the leaves, as it has not fully developed its potential for chlorophyll.

Caddy. A container for tea; can be small and brought to the table, or a large wooden box with two or three trays for mixing and blending teas. Some have extra holders, which were used for sugar, an expensive commodity in the seventeenth and eighteenth centuries. Originally, a 'catty' was a Chinese measure of weight, about 600g (1⅓lb), of tea.

Camellia sinensis. The evergreen bush from which all true tea comes. Can grow to more than 30 feet tall, but constant plucking keeps the bushes short and full, providing more leaves for tea. For premium tea, only the top two leaves and the bud leaf are picked. The next two leaves, called pouchong and souchong, are also used, and are known for more substantial, heartier flavour than the delicate top leaves. The variety of tastes depends on the altitude where it is grown, the soil, the season and the critical processing techniques.

GLOSSARY

Cha. The Japanese and the Chinese word for tea, although each language has many other words for tea; for example, Chinese has 108. O-cha is an honorific reference to tea in Japanese.

Chado. Japanese word for The Way of Tea.

Chai. Indian word for tea.

Chajin. Japanese word for teamen.

Chanoyu. Japanese word that literally means 'hot water for tea'; it is also translated as tea ceremony or tea cult. More than twenty schools of chanoyu have developed over the centuries, and ceremonies themselves differ from very simple to hours-long, elaborate performances in which both host and guests play pivotal roles.

Ché. Vietnamese word for tea.

Chong. See chung.

Chun. Chinese word for spring.

Chung or **Chong.** A large covered cup, used primarily as a vessel for pouring tea into small cups, and typically for brewing oolongs rather than green teas.

Chun hao. Chinese term for spring hair or fur.

Dan cha. Eighth-century style of Japanese tea-making, in which tea leaves were steamed and made into solid bricks to preserve them. The brick was boiled and ground into a flour, and then boiled again.

Down. The hairlike filaments on delicate white teas and buds that signal a delicate flavour. Sometimes referred to as hair.

Fa xiao. Chinese term for oxidation, that process in which some of the moisture content is removed by air or heat-drying to make the leaves more flexible to be shaped into various forms.

Feng. Chinese word for point or peak (as in the peak of a mountain).

First flush. A flush is a picking of the leaves; the first flush is the first picking of the season; an expression most commonly used in India and Sri Lanka.

Fujian. Province in mainland China that provides a wide range of highly aromatic teas; formerly spelt Fukien.

Gaibei. Covered cup commonly used in Taiwan.

Guangdong. Province in mainland China formerly spelt Kwangtung.

Gui hua. Chinese term for the osmanthus flower.

Guywan or gaiwan. A Chinese porcelain covered bowl, usually with matching saucer, in which tea is brewed. Can be used as a cup or serving vessel.

Hao. Chinese word for fur, one of several descriptions for the downy hairs on leaf buds, which is an indication of their youth and freshness.

Hu. Chinese word for a vessel to pour tea from; can be a pot or a chong.

Jiangsu. Province in mainland China, formerly spelt Kiangsu.

Ju hua. Chinese term for chrysanthemum flower.

Kakemono. Japanese tea caddy.

Kao. Cantonese word for baking; a term sometimes used for heating the leaves.

Koicha. Thick tea, usually made of matcha, which is foamed and whisked for formal Japanese tea gatherings.

Leaf set. A trade term that refers to the top two leaves plucked from a tea bush: the pekoe and orange pekoe leaves. A leaf set with bud would include the two leaves and the unopened leaf of the bud.

Long. Chinese word for dragon.

Long Jing. Chinese term for dragon's well. Also name for Dragonwell tea.

Meicha. Chinese word for eyebrow teas, which are small curved-shaped tea leaves that look like eyebrows.

Molihua. Chinese term for jasmine flower.

Molihua cha. Chinese term for jasmine tea.

Mount Emei. Site of famous Indian-style Buddhist Temple in Sichuan, China.

Mudan hua. Chinese term for tea shaped like the peony flower.

Mutan or mudan. Chinese tea leaves tied together with a silk thread or other leaves, to form the shape of a dried flower that, when infused, 'blossoms' to look like a peony or chrysanthemum.

Oolong (wulong). Chinese word for black dragon; a process for tea made by partially drying tea leaves midway between green and black.

Pan-firing. One of several ways in which green tea is withered in China, Japan and on organic farms in Sri Lanka and India. Experts dry the leaves in pans or huge woks heated over a fire. The processors move the leaves around constantly from one side of the pan to the other, to ensure an even drying of the leaf for both appearance and flavour.

Peony. See mutan.

Qing Ming. Chinese term for 'before the rain', a reference to the few days before the Qing Ming Festival in which the best teas are picked. After these few days, the tea is simply not satisfactory.

Qiu. Chinese word for ball; used to indicate a rolled tea, such as gunpowder.

Se. Chinese word for colour, and one of the four criteria for Dragonwell tea, which should be jade green in the dry leaf.

Second flush. A flush is a picking of the leaves; the second flush is the second picking in the season; an expression used primarily for Indian and Sri Lankan teas.

Showplace tea. Any one of hundreds of teas shaped into various forms that, when infused, blossom into the shape denoted by the name of the showplace tea. For example, plum teas infuse into the shape of a plum, strawberry teas infuse into the shape of a strawberry. They are not flavoured or scented unless specifically noted as such; the names generally refer only to the fruit or flower shape.

Sichuan. Province of mainland China famous for its teas; formerly spelt Szechuan.

Steamed or **steamed fired.** One of several ways green tea is withered. Experts steam the leaves in bamboo baskets over pots of spring water to gently wilt them before redrying and sorting. This process helps retain a great deal of the colour and flavour of the green leaf.

Sweet. Common word used to describe that taste element of some teas that is sweet, but is not to be confused with sugary sweet;

it is more like the sweetness of a fresh fruit, like a peach or plum.

Tatami. The straw mats laid on the floor of a Japanese tea room; the rooms are measured by the number of mats, e.g., a six-tatami room.

Tokonoma. The alcove in a Japanese tea room in which an object of art, a scroll of calligraphy, or a vase with a well-placed floral arrangement is displayed for the pleasure of the guests.

Tribute teas. Those extraordinary teas thought worthy of presenting to Chinese Emperors, now considered gifts to special leaders or guests of the Chinese government.

Usucha. Japanese foamy green tea, usually made of matcha, for light tea.

Wade-Giles spellings. The Anglican spellings of Chinese words originated in 1859 by British diplomat Sir Thomas Wade, and modified in 1892 by the scholar Herbert A. Giles.

Wei. Chinese word for taste, one of the criteria for a good tea, especially Dragonwell.

Xiang. Chinese word for aroma, one of the criteria for a good tea, especially Dragonwell.

Xing. Chinese word for shape, one of the criteria for a good tea, especially a Dragonwell.

Ye. Chinese word for leaf.

Yin. Chinese word for silver.

Yin hao. Chinese term for silver hair or fur.

Yun wu. Chinese term for clouds and mist.

Zhejiang. Province in mainland China formerly spelt Chekiang.

Resources

There's a great deal of fine sentiment in a chest of tea.
Ralph Waldo Emerson

Organisations

The Tea Council Ltd., Sir John Lyon House, 5 High Timber Street, London EC4V 3NJ.
Tel: 020 7248 1024. Fax: 020 7329 4568.
e-mail: tea@teacouncil.co.uk
Websites: www.teacouncil.co.uk   www.teahealth.co.uk
Marketing organisation for the tea trade, with over 40 member companies. Does generic promotions and commissions research reports on the health benefits of tea-drinking.

The Tea Board of India. India House, Aldwych, London WC2B 4NA.
Tel: 020 7240 2394. Fax: 020 7240 2533
Marketing organisation for importers of Indian teas.

Museum

Bramah Museum of Tea and Coffee, 1 Maguire Street, London SE1 2NQ.
Tel: 020 7378 0222. Fax: 020 7378 0219
Situated on the south side of the River Thames at Butlers Wharf near Tower Bridge, tells the story of tea and coffee in Europe over four hundred years through exhibits of ceramics, silver and graphic arts.

GREEN TEA

Traditional leaf teas served in the tea room, and a retail shop sells teas, caddies, tea strainers and tea towels. Open 10 a.m.–6 p.m. every day except Christmas Day and Boxing Day. Admission charge.

Retail and mail-order suppliers

Matthew Algie & Co. Ltd., Espresso Warehouse, 8–10 Lawmoor Road, Glasgow G6 0UL.
Tel: 0141 420 2422. Fax: 0141 420 2399
Web: www.espressowarehouse.com.uk
Green tea by mail order, including flavoured and scented teas.

Brodie Melrose Drysdale & Co. Ltd., Dock Street, Leith, Edinburgh EH6 6EY.
Tel: 0131 554 6331. Fax: 0131 555 2584.
e-mail: enquiries@brodiemelrose.com.uk
Suppliers of gunpowder teas by mail order.

The Clipper Tea Club, Clipper Teas, Broadwindsor Road, Beaminster, Dorset DT8 3PR.
Tel: 01308 863344. Web address: http://www.clipper-teas.com
Suppliers of organic teas available through retail outlets and also to club members as special offers.

The Drury Tea and Coffee Company Ltd., 37 Drury Lane, London WC2B 5RR. Tel: 020 7836 2607
Specialist retail outlet with two other London branches.

Fortnum & Mason plc, 181 Piccadilly, London W1A 1ER.
Tel: 020 7734 8040. Fax: 020 7437 3278
Department store specialising in high-quality provisions. Sells range of green teas and offers mail-order service.

The Freshly Roasted and Organic Tea and Coffee Plant, 170 Portobello Road, London W11 2EB.
Tel: 020 7221 8137. Web: www.coffee.uk.com

RESOURCES

Shop and mail-order supplier selling wide range of Chinese, Japanese and Indian teas.

The Hampstead Tea and Coffee Company Ltd., 49 Rotherwick Road, London NW11 7DR.
Tel: 020 8731 9833. Fax: 020 8458 3947
Web: www.hampsteadtea.com
Mail-order suppliers of organic teas.

Harrods Ltd., Knightsbridge, London SW1X 7XL.
Tel: 020 7730 1234 ext. 4848.
Harrods Direct Mail (for orders from catalogue): Tel: 020 7730 1234 ext. 4492.
The Food Hall sells a wide range of teas. Organic green Darjeeling tea is available by mail order.

Kamet Ltd., Dale Street, Bilston, West Midlands WV14 7JY.
Tel: 01902 403662. Fax: 01902 401212
Suppliers of Chinese green tea. No established mail-order service but will fulfil orders on request.

Netherbourne Foods Ltd., Unit 7, Irfon Business Community, Builth Wells, Powys LD2 3NL.
Tel: 01982 552012. Fax: 01982 552118.
e-mail: netherbourne.foods@virgin.net
Mail-order suppliers of gunpowder teas and can also fulfil special orders of other specific teas.

Norfolk Tea and Coffee Company Ltd., The Tea and Coffee Shop, 33 Orford Place, Norwich NR1 3QA.
Tel: 01603 760790
Retail outlet selling Chinese green teas. Also small mail-order service.

GREEN TEA

Northern Tea Merchants, Crown House, 193 Chatsworth Road, Chesterfield S40 2BA.
Tel: 01246 232600. Fax: 01246 555991.
e-mail: rbr75@dial.tipex.com
Chinese gunpowder tea available from their shop at the above address.

Pure India Tea Club, PO Box 3888, London NW9 0QF.
Tel: 020 8905 0565
Mail-order supplier of Indian teas, including green tea.

Speciality Teas and Spices, 45 Curzon Avenue, Stanmore, Middlesex HA7 2AL.
Tel: 020 8424 8521. Fax: 020 8424 2865
Mail-order supplier of Indian green teas.

Bettys by Post, at Taylors of Harrogate, Prospect Road, Harrogate, North Yorkshire HG2 7NX.
Tel: 01423 889822
Indian green teas available by mail order.

The Tea House, 15 Neal Street, London WC2H 9PU.
Tel: 020 7240 7539
Specialist retail supplier of fine teas.

T. Twining & Co. Ltd., 216 The Strand, London WC2R 1AP.
Tel: 020 7353 3511
Chinese green teas available from their shop at the above address and also supplied by mail order. They also sell teas by Jacksons of Piccadilly and Nambarrie Tea Ltd. Both Jacksons and Twinings teas are on sale in many good grocers and department store food halls.

Whittard of Chelsea
Chain of tea and coffee houses throughout London, where customers can sample teas and also buy tea, coffee and the utensils that go with them. Mail-order service available from:

RESOURCES

Whittard Direct, 73 Northcote Road, London SW11 6PJ.
Tel: 020 7924 1895. Fax: 020 7924 3085.
e-mail: direct@whittard.co.uk

George Williamson & Co., 7 Portland Close, Houghton Regis, Dunstable, Bedfordshire LU5 5AW.
Tel: 01582 813813. Fax: 01582 813811
Chinese green teas available by mail order, including hyacinth and jasmine varieties.

Windmill Tea Company, 51 Leslie Park Road, Croydon, Surrey CR0 6TP. Tel: 020 8655 3608. Fax: 020 8655 1572
Green Chinese, Japanese and Ceylon teas available retail. Orders can be supplied by mail-order on request.

Urasenke School

Mr Kimura. The Urasenke Foundation, 4 Langton Way, London SE3 7TL.
Tel: 020 8853 2595

Green tea supplements suppliers

The Nutri Centre, 7 Park Crescent, London W1N 3HE.
Tel: 020 7436 5122. Fax: 020 76360276. e-mail: nutricen@aol.com
Can supply a range of green tea supplements by different manufacturers, either in capsule or tablet form. Can be bought on the premises or supplied by mail order.

Quest Vitamins Ltd., Venture Way, Aston Science Park, Birmingham B7 4AP.
Tel: 0121 359056
Will be happy to supply their own green tea supplements by mail order.

Health and beauty products

Cosmetics and beauty aids by such companies as Revlon and Estee Lauder are available from the beauty counters of department stores. Body Shop sells its own range at its many branches, and many smaller producers have products that can be found in chemists and health food shops.

Recommended Reading

Books

Bersten, Ian B. Com (ecs). *Coffee Floats, Tea Sinks: Through History and Technology to a Complete Understanding.* Sydney: Helion Books, 1993.

Blofield, John. *The Chinese Art of Tea.* London: Allen & Unwin, 1985.

Chow, Kit, and Ione Kramer. *All the Tea in China.* San Francisco: China Books, 1990.

Evans, John C. *Tea in China, The History of China's National Drink*, London: Greenwood Press, 1992.

de Garis, Frederick. *We Japanese, Volume One.* Hakone: Fujiya Hotel, Ltd., 1934.

Gardella, Robert. *Harvesting Mountains: Fujian and the China Tea Trade, 1757–1937.* London: Greenwood Press, 1994.

Hesse, Eelco. *Tea: The Eyelids of Bodhidharma.* Reprint, Dorchester: Prism Press, 1982.

Manchester, Carole. *Tea in the East.* New York: Hearst Books, 1996.

Mitscher, Lester A., and Victoria Dolby. *The Green Tea Book: China's Fountain of Youth.* Garden City Park: Avery Publishing Group, 1998.

Okakura, Kakuzo. *The Book of Tea.* Edinburgh and London: N. Foulis, 1919.

Pettigrew, Jane. *The Tea Companion.* London: Apple, 1997.

Pratt, James Norwood, and Diana Rosen. *The Tea Lover's Companion.* Secaucus, NJ: Birch Lane Press, 1996.

Sadler, A. L. *Cha-No-Yu, The Japanese Tea Ceremony.* London: Kegan Paul & Co., 1934.

Sen, Soshitsu XV., *Tea Life, Tea Mind.* Tokyo and New York: Weatherhill, 1979.

Suzuki, Daisetz T. *Zen and Japanese Culture*. Henley on Thames: Routledge & Kegan Paul, 1982.

Ukers, William H. *All About Tea, Volumes I and II*. 1935. Reprint, Westport: Hyperion Press, 1994.

——, *The Romance of Tea: An Outline History of Tea and Tea-Drinking through Sixteen Hundred Years*. London: Alfred A. Knopf, 1936.

Vitell, Bettina. *The World in a Bowl of Tea: Healthy Seasonal Foods Inspired by the Japanese Way of Tea*. New York: Harper-Collins Publishers, 1997.

Yu, Lu. *The Classic of Tea, Origins and Rituals*. Translated by Francis Ross Carpenter, 1974. Reprint, Hopewell: The Ecco Press, 1997.

Articles

Cao, Y. and Cao, R. 'Angiogenesis inhibited by drinking tea'. *Nature*, vol. 398, p. 381 (1 April 1999).

Lin, Diana, 'Tools of the Chinese Connoisseur.' *The Free China Journal* 14, no. 28 (18 July 1997): 5.

Tea Council of Great Britain. 'Summary, Tea and Health: A Report on the Influence of Tea Drinking on the Nation's Health.' Report (November 1996).

Tufts University. 'Reading Tea Leaves for Health Benefits.' *Diet & Nutrition Letter, Special Report* 13, no. 8 (October 1995).

University of California at Berkeley. *University of California at Berkeley Wellness Letter* 10, no. 12 (September 1994).